Fine
Machine
Sewing

Fine Machine Sewing

Easy ways to get the look of hand finishing and embellishing

Carol Laflin Ahles

The Taunton Press

Cover photo: **Marcus Tullis**

Taunton
BOOKS & VIDEOS

for fellow enthusiasts

First printing: 1996
Printed in the United States of America

A THREADS Book

THREADS® is a trademark of The Taunton Press, Inc., registered in the
U.S. Patent and Trademark Office.

The Taunton Press, 63 South Main Street, Box 5506, Newtown, CT 06470-5506

Library of Congress Cataloging-in-Publication Data

Ahles, Carol.
    Fine machine sewing : easy ways to get the look of hand finishing
and embellishing / Carol Laflin Ahles.
        p.   cm.
    "A Threads book."
    Includes index.
    ISBN 1-56158-153-4
    1. Machine sewing.   I. Title.
TT713.A37   1996   96-2876
646.2—dc20   CIP

Acknowledgments

My sincere thanks to:

my husband, Ron; our children, Daniel and Emily; and our families, the Laflins and Ahleses, for their constant support and understanding;

my friends, especially Lydia Johnson, with whom I learned smocking, heirloom sewing, and much more; and Robbie Fanning for her inspiration and guidance;

the sewing educators who have taught me and those with whom I now teach for sharing their joy and excitement in sewing;

those I have taught for their enthusiasm, which makes what I do such a pleasure;

Ann Henderson at *Creative Needle* magazine and the *Threads* magazine editors with whom I have worked for encouraging my contributions to their wonderful magazines;

Eileen Hanson, Suzanne LaRosa, and Ruth Dobsevage at The Taunton Press for all their assistance with this book.

I would also like to thank the following companies and their representatives for their support and willingness to answer my questions about their products:

Sewing-machine companies—
Gayle Hillert and Shae Cox at Bernina;
Jane Burbach and Larry Diekman at Elna;
Sue Thornton-Gray and Chip Yardley at New Home;
Laura Haynie, Philip Pepper, and Louise Gerigk at Pfaff;
Sue Hausmann at Viking.

Thread, needle, lace, and stabilizer companies—
Kitty Weiland and Ken Moore at American & Efird Inc. (Mettler thread);
Gil Elzweig and Joyce Oakley at Capitol Imports (lace and fabric);
Meta Hoge at Coats & Clark;
Lisa Shepard at Handler Textile Corp.;
Rhonda Cain at SCS - U.S.A. (Madeira thread);
Gerd Boldt and Roger McClanahan at Schmetz Needle Corp.;
Fred Drexler at Sulky of America.

Contents

Introduction   2

1 Getting the Best Results   4

2 Easy Ways to Achieve Precision in Your Sewing   26

3 Decorative Edges and Creative Appliqué   42

4 Twin-Needle Stitching   52

5 Hemstitching   66

6 Fagoting   100

7 Hemming and Re-hemming, Plain or Fancy   114

8 Narrow Hemming   126

What to Look for in a Sewing Machine   142

Caring for Your Sewing Machine   145

Resources   146

Machine Settings for Decorative Techniques   147

Index   149

Introduction

This book is for all sewers who want high-quality machine stitching, finishing, and embellishing without headaches, whatever their level of expertise.

Whether I am teaching at a sewing seminar in Greensboro, North Carolina, or Kyabram, Victoria, Australia, I find that many of the frustrations experienced by machine sewers are universal. It is easy for me to empathize. I can remember years of:
• fighting puckered seams and tunneled decorative stitching, especially on lightweight fabrics (was my sewing machine a lemon or was "automatic, self-adjusting tension" a hoax?);
• estimating seam-allowance and topstitching spacing (and living with less than perfect results) because I thought being precise would be too time-consuming;
• thinking that the only applications where I would consider built-in decorative stitches would be craft projects or children's playclothes;
• trying to copy by machine the classic look of hand techniques such as hemstitching, fagoting, decorative edgings, pintucks, and shadow work, but finding both the process and the results unsatisfactory;
• struggling to machine stitch blind hems and narrow hems that would be acceptable for something other than curtains.

Like most sewers, I blamed most of these difficulties on my sewing machine. Then, in 1981, my friend Lydia Johnson and I bought Buttons 'n' Bows, a three-year-old sewing-machine dealership/fabric store in Houston that specialized in smocking and heirloom sewing. I started teaching machine classes to sewers who, like us, not only sought perfection in their sewing, but also were stitching on some of the most difficult and sheer fabrics. I researched, attended seminars, experimented, and refined, until little by little everything started to fit together. It was such a relief to learn that these common problems do not have to be inherent in machine sewing! My classes grew. I started teaching nationally, then internationally, and wrote for *Creative Needle* and then *Threads* magazines. (Some of the material in this book first appeared in my articles for these magazines.) I have now taught over 5,000 students at seminars, and have learned from them too. In this book, I'll share this know-how with you.

Chapter 1 explains how to control the factors that affect all machine sewing in order to get the best results with everything you stitch. (Demystifying tension alone will allow more control over your sewing results than you probably thought possible!) This chapter also covers sewing with lightweight fabrics and stitching buttonholes, common areas of difficulty. Chapter 2 explains ways to achieve precise, accurate, professional-looking results with much less effort than you might have expected.

The balance of the book presents fine finishing and embellishing techniques for creating useful, classic details such as pintucks, hemstitching, and fagoting. These details, which are achievable on most sewing machines, can be seen on fine ready-to-wear garments and home linens. Appropriate areas for these techniques, such as collars, pockets, cuffs, and hems, can always be found on patterns as well as on purchased garments. (In this book, pattern information for photographed garments is given only for specialized patterns.) The refinements you will learn for blind hemming and narrow hemming will give you skills you can use in finishing almost any garment. To help with problem solving, each chapter ends with related questions and answers. For decorative techniques, stitch numbers and settings for some machines are provided on pp. 147-148.

The goal of this book is to get the most from the sewing machine you have, but "What to Look for in a Sewing Machine," on pp. 142-144, addresses the question of purchasing a machine for this type of work. It explains the features I look for most and their benefits (it will also help you understand features you may already have on your machine). "Caring for Your Sewing Machine," on pp. 145-146, covers maintenance, as well as power surges, magnetic pincushions and transporting your machine.

For years I have been asked to write a comprehensive book that includes the material from my magazine articles and classes. My hope is that *Fine Machine Sewing* will open useful and creative options for you and enable you to get greater joy than ever from all your machine sewing.

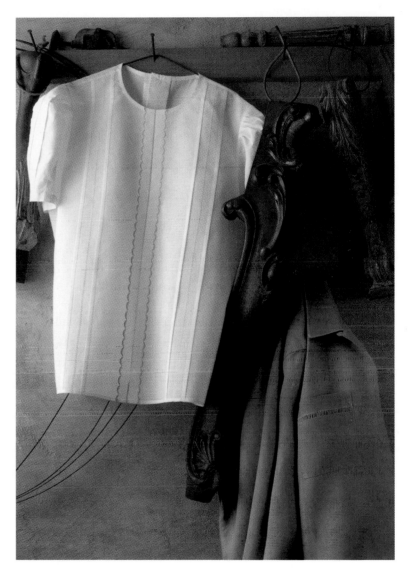

1 *Getting the Best Results*

The gentle curves of the collar are traced with decorative topstitching using the Parisian hemstitch. The folded tucks, topstitched with the Parisian hemstitch, add textural interest to this beautiful batiste blouse.

Puckered seams and tunneled decorative stitching are not an inevitable aspect of machine sewing, even with fine, lightweight fabrics. When sewers encounter such typical difficulties, their first instinct is often to blame the sewing machine, specifically its tension mechanisms. But no machine, whether an older basic mechanical machine or a new top-of-the-line computerized model, can give its best performance if it is full of lint or is being used with cheap, uneven thread, a bad needle, the wrong presser foot, or the wrong settings. If you sew only on sturdy fabrics such as denim and you are not bothered by less than perfect results, it's possible to get by with less than ideal conditions. But when you want beautiful results on the more difficult lightweight fabrics, every factor is critical—machine condition, fabric preparation, thread, bobbins, needles, presser feet, settings, and finally, tension. With these correct, "tension headaches" will become a thing of the past.

Condition of the machine

Keeping your machine clean and oiled (if oiling is recommended for the make and model you have) is one of the most important things you can do to maintain high-quality stitching as well as to avoid expensive, time-consuming repairs. Lint, especially in the top and bobbin tension areas, is a prime cause of tension problems.

Before starting a sewing project, clean your machine following the instructions in your sewing-machine manual. If you do this regularly, it takes only a few minutes—a worthwhile investment to avoid possible problems. For more detailed information on machine care, including cleaning, storing, and transporting, see pp. 145-146.

When you have stitching problems, such as skipped stitches, follow the troubleshooting routine described in the sidebar at left.

Fabric preparation

Proper preparation of the fabric is essential. For the best results, most fabrics should be prewashed. Also, take grain direction into consideration when setting up your machine. Before starting your project, sew test samples to be sure that everything is in order.

Troubleshooting

If you have stitching problems, try the measures listed here. Also refer to the problem-solving section of your sewing-machine manual.

1. Turn off the machine, then turn it back on. This resets the machine. If the problem remains, perform the following corrective measures:

2. Unthread the machine.

3. Remove the bobbin.

4. Clean the machine. Oil, if required for that model.

5. Insert a new, good-quality needle of appropriate type and size.

6. Replace the bobbin carefully.

7. Rethread carefully.

PREWASHING

Most washable fabrics should be pre-washed the same way the completed garment or project will be washed. This preshrinks the fabric, releases excess dye, and removes the sizing from the fabric surface. Why do we remove sizing when we usually want the fabric to have body? Because the difficulty in penetrating such resins can lead to problems such as skipped stitches and puckering. It is better to prewash, then spray-starch and press.

GRAIN DIRECTION

Grain direction often contributes to the problem of puckering. You can expect to have more difficulty when stitching woven fabrics in a lengthwise direction (parallel to the selvage), because lengthwise threads are stronger and have less give than crossgrain threads. You may have noticed that it is lengthwise decorative stitching and the side and center-back seams that pucker most. The photo at right shows an example of puckered lengthwise stitching and unpuckered crossgrain stitching sewn with exactly the same settings.

Should you change the grain direction when cutting the pattern pieces to avoid this problem? No, unless you are making something that will not be worn, such as a craft project. A garment may not fit or hang properly if the grain direction is changed. What you can do is use more care whenever you stitch lengthwise. For example, you may have to hold the fabric more taut as you stitch and you may have to loosen upper tension, even if this was not necessary when stitching crossgrain (selvage to selvage).

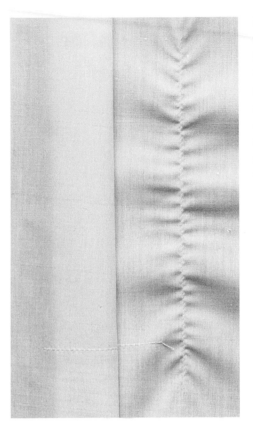

Lengthwise stitching (the vertical stitching on this sample) is naturally more likely to pucker than crossgrain stitching (the horizontal stitching). When stitching lengthwise, every factor is critical. Sewing taut and loosening upper tension may be necessary.

STITCHING TEST SAMPLES

Always take a few minutes to stitch test samples of any decorative stitching (and of straight stitching as well if you are using a fabric you are not used to), before stitching the actual project. If you don't first perfect the stitching on a test sample, you may have to live with less than satisfactory results on the project or rip out your work and start again, both of which are time-consuming and frustrating. Stitch with conditions exactly the same as will exist on the project, including the thread, needle, grain direction, number of fabric layers, stabilizer, and so on. Note any necessary adjustments (including tension) right on the fabric sample, and save it in a notebook for future reference (see the sidebar on p. 8).

Making a sample notebook

One of my most valuable machine-sewing references is a notebook that contains samples of all my favorite techniques (see the photo at right). When I am planning a project, my notebook provides inspiration. And in the long run, keeping samples saves time. Each sample has the appropriate presser foot, stitch numbers, settings, and so on, written right on it; so I don't have to remember what I did the last time or retry all the possible variables for every technique.

I recommend that you stitch and save practice samples of any technique in this book that interests you. Use a ball-point pen to note thread, needle, presser foot, stitch number, stitch width and length, upper-tension adjustment, guiding aids, and so on, directly on the fabric pieces. I mark the stitch combinations I like best with a star. Include any information that will help to repeat this technique on your particular machine. Attach your practice pieces and notes to sturdy three-hole paper or slip them into plastic pocket pages and keep them in a three-ring binder. Add to your notebook as you experiment with other techniques on your machine. As it grows, it will become a valuable source of information.

A notebook containing practice samples is a valuable reference. All pertinent information should be noted directly on the fabric. You can star favorite combinations.

Thread

If you are looking for top-quality results, start with good-quality thread. Choose thread that is appropriate to the stitching technique (generally seam stitching versus decorative stitching) and the fabric (for example, for fine fabric, choose fine thread). Don't waste your time and risk good results by using cheap thread with nubs, uneven thickness, or fuzziness.

In general, extra-fine cotton-wrapped polyester thread is appropriate for seaming most light- to medium-weight fabrics. Fine mercerized cotton can be used on fine, all-natural wovens if strength is not needed. For more strength on heavier fabrics, use long-staple polyester. For decorative stitching on light- to medium-weight fabrics, use fine machine-embroidery thread, usually cotton (size 50/2 or 60/2) or rayon (size 40).

Often more than one thread is used on a single garment. For example, a fine, machine-embroidery cotton thread might be used for the decorative stitching on a batiste or broadcloth blouse, while extra-fine cotton-wrapped polyester thread would be used to construct it.

Naturally, thread selection involves personal preference and is necessarily influenced by availability. The main threads used in machine sewing are cotton, polyester, and cotton-wrapped polyester; rayon, metallic, silk, and other specialty threads are also available. If you can't find them locally, most may be mail-ordered from the sources listed on p. 146.

COTTON THREAD

Cotton thread easily produces an attractive stitch (this is why dealers use it to demonstrate sewing machines). It has some sheen, but relatively little strength and stretch. Thread comes in various "sizes"—the higher the size number, the finer the thread. If there is a second number, it indicates the number of plies. Machine-embroidery thread is usually two-ply, and all-purpose cotton thread is three-ply. For example, 60/2 indicates a fine, machine-embroidery two-ply thread, and 50/3 a medium, all-purpose three-ply thread.

Machine-embroidery cotton thread is excellent for decorative stitching (including satin stitching for appliquéing and buttonholes), but is generally not strong enough for seaming. All-purpose cotton thread can be used to seam all-natural woven fabrics, but I rarely use it on garments since I find it too bulky for lightweight fabrics and not strong enough for heavier ones. It is often used for piecing quilts, though. Do not use cotton thread to seam swimwear or most knits.

Recommended brands of cotton thread include DMC, Madeira, Mettler, and Zwicky.

POLYESTER THREAD

Polyester thread is strong and has some stretch. Good-quality (long-staple), fine polyester thread provides strength without bulk for seaming most medium- to heavy-weight wovens, as well as knits and swimwear. Polyester thread is not generally recommended for decorative stitching.

Although a different sizing system is used for polyester thread (size 100 polyester is not as fine as size 100 cotton), the rule is still, "the higher the number, the finer the thread." Polyester thread size 100 is the fine weight usually preferred. If there is no size given on a polyester thread, unwrap a few inches and check the size visually.

Recommended brands of polyester thread include Gutermann, Metrosene Plus (from Mettler), and Molnlycke.

COTTON-WRAPPED POLYESTER THREAD

Cotton-wrapped polyester combines the nice sheen of cotton with the strength of a polyester core. It is available in all-purpose and extra-fine weights. No size numbers are given. The all-purpose weight can be used on heavier fabrics, where the bulk of the thread is not a problem. The extra-fine weight (such as Coats Dual Duty Plus extra fine) is excellent for seaming light- to medium-weight fabrics and for blind hemming. Extra-fine white can be used on all light pastel colors.

SPECIALTY THREADS

Rayon threads (such as Madeira Rayon and Sulky) and metallic threads are for decorative stitching only. Some silk threads are recommended for hand sewing only, while others are designed for machine sewing. Buttonhole twist, topstitching thread, and cordonnet (on spools) are all different names for the same product. These heavy threads are

If the thread spool has a slit to hold the thread tail, put the spool on the machine with the slit to the right (toward the flywheel) on horizontal spool pins and down on vertical spool pins. This prevents the thread from catching on the slit.

Thread the machine with the presser foot up so that the tension discs are not engaged. You can lower the presser foot when threading the needle, though. Many machines have a light color behind the needle to make threading easier.

used for topstitching, very heavy-duty utility sewing, or possibly, for some open (not dense) decorative machine stitching for a bold look on medium- to heavy-weight fabrics. In fine machine sewing, these threads are used mostly for cording buttonholes or for decorative stitching (as is pearl cotton) to add strength and a more finished appearance.

Many new special-purpose threads have become available in the last few years. Check thread labels and the information on thread displays for suggested uses for particular products.

Bobbins

For seaming, use the same thread on the bobbin as on the top. For decorative stitching, you can use a different thread on the bobbin for convenience and economy, as long as you adjust upper tension to compensate. For example, when decorative stitching with rayon thread, for the bobbin you might prefer a fine cotton thread in a color that matches the fabric, in order to save the time and expense of changing bobbins each time the top color is changed. Since with decorative stitching it is desirable for the upper thread to be pulled slightly to the underside, you may have to loosen upper tension, depending on the type and weight of thread used.

When winding the bobbin with any thread that stretches, such as polyester, wind at a slow to medium speed to reduce potential puckering later.

I store each bobbin together with the thread spool from which it was wound. There are several easy ways to accomplish this. With most thread-spool racks, you can place the bobbin on a spool holder, then put the thread spool on top of it on the same holder. For taller thread spools, you can extend the length

of the spool holder with a drinking straw cut to the desired length. If the bobbins will not fit over the straw, hammer a small nail near each spool holder for the corresponding bobbin. You can also buy plastic bobbin holders that fit on the center of most thread spools to hold the corresponding bobbin.

Even with these strategies, bobbins sometimes get separated from the spools. Therefore, I label bobbins with an extra-fine permanent marker, as you can see in the photo on the facing page. (The marking can be removed with alcohol when necessary.) Marking takes only a few seconds and saves the time and aggravation of having to guess. Abbreviate the thread type and size (for example, "Met 60" for Mettler size 60 cotton) and write the color number below. This information will fit between the holes on bobbins, if necessary, and is especially helpful when you have several different types and sizes of the same color thread, such as white. Avoid labeling bobbins with hole reinforcers or tape because either the label itself or the its sticky residue can impede thread movement.

Following are some additional tips regarding bobbins that will help avoid problems and ensure successful sewing:
• Use only bobbins recommended for that machine.
• Use only bobbins in good condition—not bent, and without rough spots.
• Invest in a good supply of bobbins so you always have an empty one on hand.
• Make sure no loose threads or thread loops are hanging from the bobbin. (After you've begun winding a bobbin, stop and cut the thread tail close to the bobbin, then continue to wind.)
• Avoid winding one thread over another on a bobbin. The outside thread may not wind as evenly or as tightly as it should. Furthermore, when you get to

the end of the outside thread, a tail from the inside thread can come loose and cause problems such as jamming.

• Make sure to insert the bobbin into the bobbin case in the right direction and to "click" the thread into the bobbin tension device. If you just drag the bobbin thread across the bobbin tension slit, you may be sewing without bobbin tension.

• Don't use a metal tool to bring up the bobbin thread, as it can scratch the needle plate. Instead, pass a length of thread or a piece of fabric under the presser foot to catch the bobbin thread.

Needles

After you've made your thread selection, choose a needle appropriate for that thread and the fabric. You can find thread and needle charts in most sewing-machine manuals and machine-sewing books. In general, fabric, thread, and needle must all correlate—for a fine lightweight fabric, use a fine thread and a fine (small) needle. For some techniques, such as twin-needle stitching and hemstitching, you need special-purpose needles (see pp. 54-55 and pp. 68-69, respectively).

Use good-quality needles—Schmetz or the brand recommended by your machine dealer. A dull, damaged, or poor-quality needle will affect stitch quality and can also cause puckers and damaged fabric.

Needles with Universal points produce good results on most fabrics. (Happily this is the least expensive needle type, and a good supply of Universals will cover most needs.) Usually, you need to switch to a needle with a special point or design, such as a Sharp (also called denim), stretch, or embroidery needle, only when you have stitching problems with Universal needles, which can happen on certain fabrics or with special threads. For example, if fragile decorative threads are shredding with Universal needles, try Embroidery or Metallica needles from Schmetz or Metafil needles from Lammertz, which are designed for these threads.

TIP

Sewing-machine dealers are more likely than most fabric-store chains to carry a broad range of machine needles (or to be willing to special order what they don't carry). Most needles are interchangeable from machine to machine. However, some machines, especially those more than a few years old, require special needles. If in doubt, consult your machine manual or your dealer.

The clear tops of the Schmetz boxes for Universal needles magnify. It is easier to read the size engraved on a needle if you slip the needle into one of these boxes.

With needles, the higher the number, the thicker the needle. Use the smallest size needle in the range suggested for your fabric and thread. Too large a needle causes puckering, but the needle must be large enough for the thread to slide through the eye freely and to create a hole in the fabric big enough for the thread.

Most needles are now labeled with two numbers, such as 70/10. The first number is the size at the middle of the blade in hundredths of millimeters. (This is sometimes shown with "Nm" for "number metric.") The number following the slash is the American equivalent based on Singer sizes used in the U.S. early in this century.

The needle types and sizes used most for fine machine sewing are Universal size 70/10 for batiste-weight fabrics and Universal size 80/12 for broadcloth-weight fabrics. In this book, I will refer only to the metric size, for example "70 Universal."

Generally you should replace the needle after stitching a major project. And whenever you have stitching difficulties, try a new needle. If a needle hits a pin, of course, it is damaged and should be replaced. When you start a special project, put in a new needle to ensure the best possible results—a new needle costs very little considering your investment in fabric and supplies, as well as your time for sewing. Be sure to insert the needle the right direction (for most machines, the flat side goes to the back) and all the way into the needle bar.

The best way to store needles is in the boxes they come in. These boxes are designed specifically to protect the needles from the climate, to keep them from getting bent, and to protect the points.

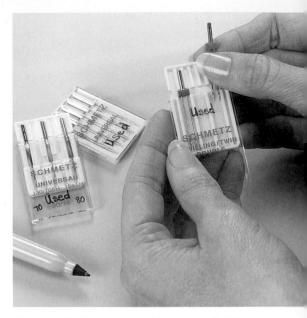

Empty needle boxes are good for storing slightly used needles. Mark the box 'used,' and include the type and size of the needle if different from the label.

Sometimes you need to replace a barely used needle with a different size or type. I store such used but still good needles in empty needle boxes. I write "used" on the box with an extra-fine marker, plus the type and size of the needle if these are different from what the label states (see the photo above). When it is not crucial that the needle be new, use one of these slightly used ones again, then discard it. Some people suggest putting used needles back in their original box with the points up (toward the top of the box), to distinguish them from the new ones, which have their points down. However, I don't recommend this practice because the grooves in the box are shaped for points down and the needles can become bent.

Presser feet

For best results, the presser foot should hold the fabric as securely as possible. This is best accomplished with a foot that is metal, that covers as much of both feed dogs as possible, and is flat on the underside. For most straight stitching, a basic metal zigzag foot adequately meets these criteria.

For any dense stitching, such as satin stitching, or any other raised effects, such as twin-needle pintucking or stitching over cord, a foot that is indented underneath is needed. Satin-stitch feet, and their variations, have grooves on the underside to let the raised stitching or fabric pass easily under the foot without becoming crushed. Do not use these feet for regular straight stitching because the indented area allows the fabric to flutter, which can cause puckering and skipped stitches. The photo at right shows zigzag and satin-stitch feet.

Unfortunately, the terminology for identifying presser feet is not uniform throughout the sewing industry. To identify the presser feet that go with your machine, you can always consult your sewing-machine manual. But understanding some of the basics about presser-foot design will help you identify feet and understand their uses no matter what the feet are called.

To some extent, presser feet are interchangeable from machine to machine. See the sidebar on p. 15 for specifics.

ZIGZAG AND SATIN-STITCH FEET

The basic zigzag and satin-stitch feet are used by far the most. The zigzag foot, also called a standard sewing foot, is usually the first foot (labeled "A" or "0") among the group that comes with the machine. It is basically flat underneath,

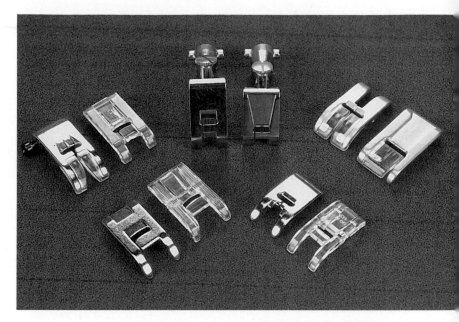

Basic zigzag feet (left foot within each pair) are best for straight stitching. Satin-stitch feet (right foot within each pair) are best for dense stitching or other raised effects.

but may be partially indented behind the needle opening and/or at the back. The satin-stitch foot, also called an appliqué, embroidery, or fancy-stitch foot, may be metal, plastic, or a combination. It should have an indented area underneath.

STRAIGHT-STITCH FEET

Straight-stitch feet, shown in the top photo on p. 14, are flat on the underside and have a hole or a very narrow opening for the needle. Thus, the only possible stitch with this type of foot is a straight stitch in center needle position. Because a straight-stitch foot holds the fabric around the needle more securely than does the basic zigzag foot, it will help reduce puckering and skipped stitches on lightweight fabrics, as well as offer more support for precision straight stitching near the edge of most fabrics. (Special straight-stitch feet for sewing ⅛ in. or ¼ in. from an edge are discussed on pp. 30-31.)

TIP

For straight stitching, use presser feet that have flat undersides and cover both feed dogs. For dense stitching or other raised effects, feet that are indented underneath are best, because the raised stitching or fabric passes easily underneath.

On machines that sew up to a maximum width of only 4mm, the feed dogs and the toes of the presser feet holding the fabric over them are closer together and hold the fabric more securely in the center than on machines that sew up to 9mm wide. If your machine has wide-set feed dogs, compensate when sewing lightweight fabric by experimenting with different feet, needle positions, and guiding so that you are stitching where the fabric is held most securely.

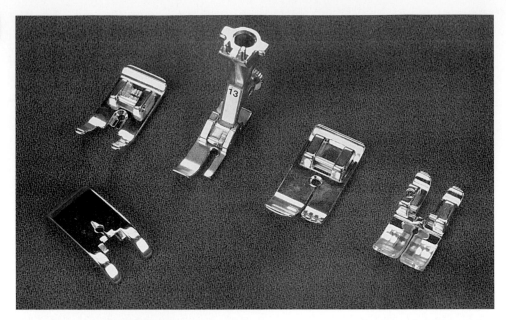

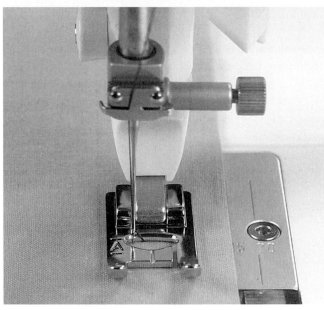

Straight-stitch feet, which are flat on the underside and have a round or very narrow opening for the needle, hold the fabric securely all around the needle.

Moving the needle position to the far left or right when using a basic metal zigzag foot simulates the support of a straight-stitch foot and helps reduce puckering and skipped stitches on lightweight fabrics.

If your seams on lightweight fabric are puckering and you do not have a straight-stitch foot, you can imitate its support when using a basic metal zigzag foot by changing the needle position to the far left or right, as shown in the photo above (see also pp. 29-30). With the needle in this position, the fabric around the needle is held firmly on three sides. With the needle in center position, the fabric immediately to each side of the needle and sometimes in front (depending on the location of the open slit) is not held very firmly. Remember to adjust your guiding to compensate for the different needle position. (On Elnas, use the sheer-fabric foot "Y," if you have it, since it is flatter underneath.)

Interchanging presser feet

If a foot design you want is not available for your machine, the foot from another brand or a generic foot may work, especially if the shank length is the same. Most newer machines are "short-shank" (also called "low-shank")—the distance from where the shank screws onto the needle bar down to the needle plate (with the presser foot lowered) is about ½ in.

If your machine is not short shank, an adaptor may be available so that you can still use other short-shank feet. For example, the shanks on Bernina machines are unique, but in the event that you want a foot not available for your Bernina, a short-shank adaptor for your particular model can be purchased from Bernina dealers. With the adaptor, you can use many short-shank feet, or a short ankle and the corresponding snap-on soles. Both Clotilde and Nancy's Notions mail-order companies (see Resources on p. 146) have adaptors to enable high-shank machines (those that measure about 1 in. from the screw to the needle plate) to use short-shank feet. I know of no adaptor for Singer models with slanted shanks.

If your machine has snap-on feet (the snap-on part is often called the sole), first check whether the sole from the other brand will snap onto your machine. If it does, lower the presser foot and carefully turn the flywheel toward you to lower the needle and then raise it to check the alignment (whether the needle hits the foot). If the sole does not fit your machine, or if it fits but the needle hits the foot, then try replacing your shank or ankle (the part that screws onto the needle bar) with an ankle from the other brand. Snap the sole onto the new ankle, lower the presser foot and check the alignment. If this ankle works, you need to purchase only one, and you will be able to use all the soles of that same brand and style. Some companies have more than one style of ankle, so if one does not work another might.

The Elna 9000 and Diva have a fixed ankle, but some other soles snap onto it and work fine. Elna's soles for these models (as well as for previous models) can be used on other brands. Several ankles are available to make a sole work on different machines.

Before stitching with a foot not designed for your machine, take the following steps:

1. Check whether the needle-hole opening is narrower than the maximum stitch width of your machine. For example, if your machine stitches 9mm wide and you try to do so using a foot with a 4mm opening (designed for machines that do not stitch as wide as yours), the needle will hit the foot and break.

2. Lower the presser foot and see how much of the feed dogs is covered by the sole. (Remember that for the best feeding and stitch quality, the sole should cover as much of the feed dogs as possible.)

3. With the needle in center-needle position, check whether the needle is centered on the foot. When an Elna pintuck sole is used on some New Home machines, for example, the twin needles do not align with the center groove of the sole. Usually the needle position can be changed to correct this misalignment.

4. Finally, when you buy a foot (or any other sewing-machine accessory, for that matter), make sure that it can be returned for a refund within a reasonable amount of time if you are not satisfied.

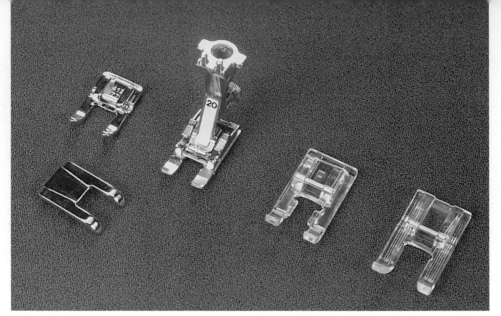

Open-toe feet provide excellent visibility during stitching but should be used only when the fabric is stabilized enough so that it is not necessary for the presser foot to keep the fabric from fluttering.

TIP

Sewers who don't have an open-toe foot sometimes create one by cutting off the center front of plastic or part-plastic satin-stitch feet up to the toe. I would recommend doing this only if you need more visibility than the transparent front of a satin-stitch foot allows, and then only if you have another satin-stitch foot to use for all other satin stitching.

OPEN-TOE FEET

Open-toe presser feet (see the photo above) are, as the name implies, completely open in front of the needle, providing excellent visibility as you sew. The drawback is that only the two "toes" extending on the sides hold the fabric in front. And since these are a variation of satin-stitch feet, the groove on the underside allows additional movement or fluttering of the fabric as you stitch.

Open-toe feet should be used only for techniques where visibility is essential and where the fabric is already sufficiently stabilized that the presser foot does not need to keep the fabric from fluttering. For example, you might use an open-toe foot for appliquéing when the fabric is in a hoop and/or has a stabilizer underneath. Unless the fabric is stabilized, puckering and tunneling are likely to occur.

OTHER USEFUL FEET

Special-purpose feet can be very helpful in certain situations. When choosing a special-purpose foot, take note of a foot's design, construction (metal versus plastic), and underside. If you keep in mind

that the fabric will be held most securely by a metal foot with the most surface covering the fabric and feed dogs, you will be able to choose the best foot for a task and to compensate when necessary.

Following are some special-purpose feet that are useful for fine machine sewing. When you need a foot for a special purpose, such as to guide fabric or cord in a certain position, consider using any foot that meets the need as long as its underside is appropriate.

Blind-hem feet The guide on a blind-hem foot (see the photo at upper left on the facing page) is helpful for blind hemming as well as for other techniques.

Buttonhole feet The two grooves under a traditional buttonhole foot (see the photo at upper right on the facing page) can be used to guide cord or small corded piping as well as to make buttonholes.

Multiple-cord feet Different configurations of holes or slots in multiple-cord feet (see the photo at lower left on the facing page) guide cord on top of the

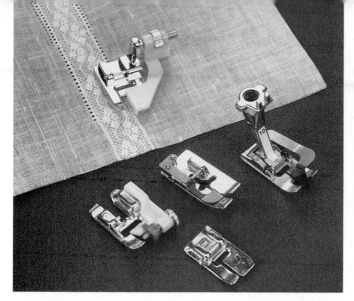

Blind-hem feet can be used for techniques such as hemstitching lace, where their guides would be helpful.

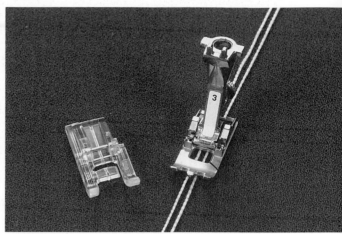

The two grooves under a traditional buttonhole foot can be used to guide cord or small corded piping.

Multiple-cord feet have holes or slots to guide cord on top of fabric. These feet are especially useful to cord hemstitching and other decorative stitches.

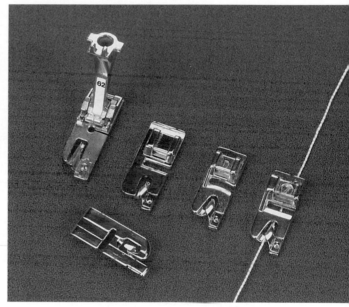

Narrow hemmers are for stitching hems 2mm to 6mm wide. They may also be used to guide a cord for stitching on top of the fabric.

fabric. These feet are especially useful for cording hemstitching and other decorative stitches. They can be used without cord as metal satin-stitch feet.

Narrow hemmers Narrow hemmers (see the photo at lower right) are used to turn and stitch hems 2mm to 6mm wide. Some can be used only with a straight stitch, others are designed to align with a zigzag stitch (these are also called rolled or shell hemmers), and some can be used with either. An alternate use for these feet is for guiding

STITCH-LENGTH CONVERSION CHART	
STITCH LENGTH IN MILLIMETERS	STITCHES PER INCH
1	25
2	12
3	8
4	6

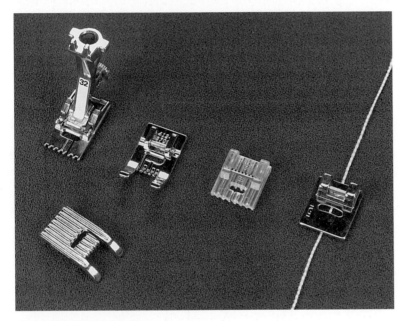

Pintuck feet have grooves underneath for forming twin-needle pintucks equidistantly spaced. The grooves can also be used to guide cord or corded edges.

cord to be stitched on top of the fabric; the cord is fed through the curl of the hemmer.

Pintuck feet Pintuck feet (see the photo above) have grooves underneath to form twin-needle pintucks and to space them equidistantly. The grooves can also be used as guides for other stitching, including for cords and corded edges. (Note: Pfaff uses the term cording feet for some of its pintuck feet.) If I have a choice, I most often use pintuck feet having seven grooves.

Try to find pintuck feet that do not have a wide center-front slit because fabric can be pulled up into this open space inconsistently.

Stitch settings

On lightweight or soft fabrics, a long stitch tends to cause puckering, and a wide stitch tends to cause tunneling. You can compensate by shortening stitch length and narrowing stitch width. Stabilizing the fabric will also help eliminate these problems, as will loosening the upper tension, as discussed on pp. 20-22.

LENGTH

For seaming lightweight fabrics, use a stitch length of approximately 2mm. If a long length is needed, as for gathering or basting, lengthen the stitch only as much as necessary, loosen upper tension, and stabilize by sewing taut. For example, to gather batiste, use a stitch length of only 3mm to 3.5mm for prettier gathers with less puckering. Loosen upper tension significantly—usually about two numbers. (The bobbin thread will be taut, which makes it easier to pull for gathering and removing later.) To sew taut, put pressure on the fabric with one hand in front of and one hand behind the presser foot as you sew, as shown in the photo at left on the facing page. Do not pull or stretch the fabric.

Stitch lengths are given in millimeters throughout the book. If your machine is marked in stitches per inch, use the conversion chart at top left.

WIDTH

For any zigzag stitch, including most decorative stitches, use a stitch width no wider than necessary. If a very wide stitch is needed, compensate for the tendency of the fabric to tunnel by stabilizing the fabric and reducing upper

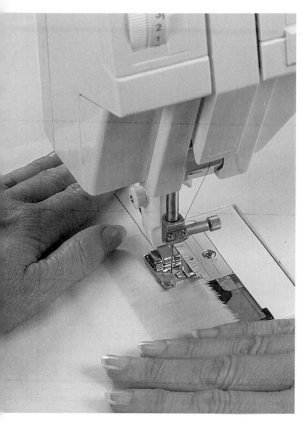

Sewing taut is one of the ways to compensate for the tendency of a long stitch to pucker. As you sew, hold the fabric taut with one hand in front of and one hand behind the presser foot; do not pull or stretch the fabric.

tension. Spray-starching and pressing stabilize the fabric somewhat; a hoop can be used when appropriate; but generally a light tearaway stabilizer should be used under any satin stitching, buttonholes, and most decorative stitching.

Stabilizers for lightweight fabrics

Thick and stiff stabilizers can distort delicate fabric or stitching when they are torn away. Lightweight fabrics call for lightweight stabilizers.

Sulky packages a lightweight tear-away stabilizer called Tear-Easy. Speed Stitch distributes two similar products

called "Soft" from Mark Textiles and "Stiff" from Handler Textile Corp., either of which is appropriate for lightweight fabric (don't be misled by the Handler product's name). Other names to look for are Jiffy Tear Away from Staple Sewing Aids Corp. and Armo Tear Away from Handler. (RinsAway from Handler is a little heavier.)

You can use multiple layers of these lightweight stabilizers when more stability is required for heavier fabrics. Some stabilizers tear more easily in one direction than another; test your stabilizer and plan its placement before you stitch.

If your favorite fabric store does not have any of these stabilizers, ask the owners if they'll consider carrying one. For mail-order sources of stabilizers, see Resources on p. 146. Tear-Easy, "Soft" from Mark Textiles, and "Stiff" from Handler Textile Corp. can be mail ordered from Speed Stitch.

Decorative machine stitchers used to use paper as a stabilizer all the time because that's all there was. Now I would use it only if I had nothing else that would work. Feed dogs cannot grip and feed slick paper as well as they can the newer stabilizers. Although this defi-

When tearing away stabilizer, hold the stitching firmly between your thumb and index finger and tear up to your thumbnail to protect the delicate stitching and fabric.

TIP

To keep delicate stitching and fabric from being distorted when tearing stabilizer away, hold the stitching between your thumb and index finger and tear the stabilizer up to your thumbnail, as shown in the photo above.

For satin stitching (and other decorative stitching), the top side of the stitch should be rounded, with no bobbin thread showing on the sides. The upper thread should be slightly pulled to the underside, as seen at left. To accomplish this, loosen upper tension so that more thread is fed into the upper side of the stitch.

ciency may not be noticeable on some stitching, it is critical when precise feeding is important, for example, on buttonholes. Sewing through paper also dulls needles quickly; they need to be changed more frequently, and before you realize that the needles have become dull, the quality of the stitching may already have deteriorated. If you must use paper, use the lightest weight that will offer enough stability.

Water-soluble stabilizers, such as Solvy, Stitch 'n' Spray, Aqua-Solv, and Avalon, do not offer enough support for most decorative stitching unless they are used in combination with a hoop. However, multiple fused layers of these water solubles work well for some techniques, such as fagoting, where other stabilizers would be difficult to tear away or would leave whiskers that would show. You can fuse two or more layers together between press cloths to add needed body and stiffness.

In recent years many other new stabilizers have been introduced, including some fusibles, some paint-on and spray-on products, and some that disintegrate with the heat of a dry iron. All have unique advantages for appropriate applications, but sometimes there are also drawbacks. It is crucial to test a product thoroughly before using it on a special project, especially a delicate one, and to follow the manufacturer's instructions carefully.

Tension

Tension is one of the least understood factors in machine sewing. While it is true that the upper tension rarely has to be adjusted for "normal sewing" (as the manuals usually say), there are many times upper tension should be changed for the best results on different fabrics and for certain techniques. Furthermore, "normal" tension on any brand or model varies from machine to machine because to a certain extent it has been set according to the judgment of the person setting the machine. If adjusting the upper tension really weren't necessary, there would not be a numbered dial so accessible on every machine!

Tension is really not so mysterious. Think of it as a way to control the amount of thread fed into each stitch. When you want more thread fed into the upper side of the stitch, loosen upper tension by adjusting the dial to a lower number or toward "minus." This is the most common adjustment. For satin stitching, for example, it is desirable to loosen upper tension slightly to put more thread on top, creating a rounded look with no bobbin thread showing on the sides, as shown in the photo at left. On some sewing machines the appropriate position for looser tension is marked on the dial (on the Bernina 1630 the dial has a gray area, and on the Elna 7000, 9000, and Diva the dials have a blue area). And the computers on some machines automatically loosen tension in certain situations; but since the automatic adjustment is an estimate, you should still stitch a test sample and understand how to adjust upper tension yourself.

Adjust tension only after checking all the other factors. For example, if you are straight stitching on fine fabric, a dirty machine, thick thread, a bad needle, the wrong foot, or a long stitch length can all cause puckering. Correct these conditions before adjusting the tension.

When tension adjustment is necessary, adjust upper tension, not bobbin tension. Once bobbin tension is set correctly, you should not have to adjust it regularly to balance the stitch. (For special effects, however, such as using thick threads on the bobbin, bobbin tension can be bypassed or loosened.)

Tension-related problems include puckering, thread breaking, and an imbalanced stitch. With a straight stitch, the top and bobbin threads should interlock between the layers of fabric, and the stitches should look the same on both sides. If upper tension is too tight, too little top thread is being fed into the stitch; the top thread will look taut and the seam will pucker, as you can see in the photo at right. Loosen upper tension to feed enough thread into each stitch so that the stitch is balanced and puckers are eliminated. In general, adjust only about one-fourth to one-half the distance from one number to the next at one time, then test again. In other words, if the dial is set at 5 and you wish to loosen upper tension, turn the dial to 4¾ or 4½ . If upper tension is too loose, the bobbin thread looks taut, and loops from the upper thread show on the back side of the fabric. Correct the problem by tightening upper tension slightly.

For a standard zigzag or a utility-type zigzag variation, such as an overlock stitch, the sides of the stitches should interlock between the fabric layers. However, for satin stitching, buttonholes, and most decorative stitching, it is desirable for the upper thread to be slightly pulled to the underside. Slightly loosening upper tension accomplishes this, creates a more rounded appearance on the right side, and reduces tunneling.

Note that any additional guide through which a thread passes puts more tension on the thread. You can use this fact to your advantage to further increase or reduce tension on the top or bobbin thread. For example, if one side of twin-needle stitching appears loose and the other appears tight, feed the loose-side thread through an additional guide at the top of the machine or on the needle bar and bypass one of these guides with the tight-side thread. To

Tension controls the amount of thread fed into each stitch. When too little thread is fed into the upper side of a straight stitch, the top thread looks taut and the seam puckers, as in the sample at left. To correct this, loosen upper tension. The sample at right shows a correctly balanced straight stitch.

increase drag on the bobbin thread to pull satin stitching and buttonhole stitching to the underside, Bernina suggests threading the bobbin thread through a hole in the finger of the bobbin case on some models.

Understanding and using the upper-tension dial enables you to fine-tune your stitching according to the fabric and the application. Adjusting upper tension enables you to:

• get the best stitch balance without puckering, especially with lengthwise stitching on difficult fabrics (in most cases loosen tension slightly; if you loosen too much the upper thread will form loops on the underside);
• create more of a raised effect on twin-needle pintucks (tighten) or reduce puckering on them (loosen);
• with hemstitching, create holes that are more visible (tighten) or reduce puckering (loosen);
• eliminate the pulling of blind hem stitches (loosen);
• keep the fabric flat when you are stitching two rows of lengthened

straight stitching for gathering (loosen) or gather ruffles automatically (tighten);
• stitch fagoting that does not pull the two sides together (loosen).

Not taking advantage of this ability to adjust upper tension is needlessly limiting. Making it work for you will make your sewing much more enjoyable.

Additional tips

Following are some additional tips for getting the best machine-sewing results:
• When beginning a line of stitching, always hold the thread tails toward the back of the machine for the first few stitches.
• Maintain a smooth, even stitching speed. Use a slow to medium speed for decorative and twin-needle stitching.
• If your machine allows for adjusting the pressure on the presser foot, consult the machine manual for the proper setting. There should be enough pressure to feed the fabric precisely, but not so much as to mar or crush the fabric.

Sewing with lightweight fabrics

Lightweight fabrics, which are often used for fine machine sewing, can be tricky to sew. Here is a checklist for getting the best results:
• Clean the machine. Then oil it, if required for that model.
• Use good-quality, fine thread. For seaming most lightweight fabrics, use extra-fine cotton-wrapped polyester thread. Fine mercerized cotton can be used on all natural wovens, if strength is not needed. For decorative stitching, use fine machine-embroidery thread, such as 50/2 or 60/2 cotton.
• Use a new, good-quality needle that is appropriate in size and kind

for the fabric and thread, most often size 70 Universal.
• Use a stitch length of about 2mm for seaming, and a stitch width that is no wider than necessary.
• For straight stitching, use the basic zigzag foot (with the needle in far left or right position, if necessary) or a straight-stitch foot. For dense stitching, use a satin-stitch foot.
• To stabilize straight stitching, sew taut with one hand in front of and one behind the presser foot. For decorative stitching or buttonholes, use a lightweight tearaway stabilizer under the fabric.
• Slightly loosening upper tension may be necessary, especially for lengthwise straight stitching or any decorative stitching.
• Press each seam flat, then press open or as desired.
• Test your stitching on scraps first.

BUTTONHOLES

Buttonhole stitching problems are common on lightweight fabrics. Remember that a buttonhole is really two rows of satin stitching, so in general most of the rules for satin stitching apply.
• Use fine thread. Both good-quality size 50/2 or 60/2 machine-embroidery cotton thread and extra-fine cotton-wrapped polyester thread make attractive buttonholes on lightweight fabrics.
• Use a good-quality needle appropriate in type and size for the fabric and thread. It must be in good condition. If in doubt, use a new needle.
• Since interfacing is rarely used on sheer fabrics, you need a lightweight tearaway stabilizer underneath buttonholes. Carefully tear it away after stitching.
• If your machine has a sewing table, use it. The larger working surface will give more control.

• Slightly loosening upper tension will create a smoother satin stitch and help reduce both puckering and tunneling.

• Use a smooth, even, slow to medium sewing speed. (Use the "slow" button if the machine has one.)

• Avoid making buttonholes thick and dense, especially on lightweight fabric. For more strength, cord buttonholes with buttonhole twist or pearl cotton rather than making them denser.

• Stitch several test samples with exactly the same conditions as exist on the garment, including grain direction, number of layers, interfacing or stabilizer, and so on. Follow instructions in your machine manual for any adjustments necessary.

• Keep in mind that any change in conditions can affect one or both sides of the buttonhole. For example, one buttonhole stitched over additional thicknesses of fabric (as on the seam allowance where a gathered skirt is attached to a yoke) might require additional adjustment. Always grade such areas to eliminate as much bulk as possible.

Questions

How can I keep from cutting through the ends of buttonholes when cutting them open?

Most experts cut buttonholes with a buttonhole chisel and wooden block. To cut buttonholes smaller than the ½-in. chisel, place one of the bar tacks just beyond the edge of the block.

If you do not have a buttonhole chisel, use a sharp seam ripper to cut carefully from one end of the buttonhole just to the middle. Then cut from the other end to the middle. As a precaution, you can put pins across each end of the buttonhole, just inside the bar tack.

Buttonholes made with fine machine-embroidery cotton thread (size 50 to 60) are attractive, but are they strong enough for stress areas, such as the shoulder on jumpers and jumpsuits? Should I use a heavier thread or stitch around the buttonhole twice in these areas?

Using heavier thread or stitching the buttonhole twice would add too much bulk but little strength. To add strength without bulk, simply cord buttonholes with pearl cotton, buttonhole twist, top-stitching thread, and so on. Match the cord color to the thread color.

Many machine manuals have instructions for cording buttonholes. Either catch the cord over a prong and into the slits of a buttonhole foot designed for this cording, or lay the cord under the two grooves of other buttonhole feet, with the loop to the back in most cases. Position the fabric so that the loop is toward the outside edge of the garment (on jumpers, this is toward the top of the garment), and stitch the buttonhole over the cord.

After stitching, pull the cord tails until the loop is hidden. Then, using a needle threader, thread the tails into a hand sewing needle with a large eye, take them to the underside, knot them together, bury a small length of the tails, and cut off the excess.

Whenever I try to stitch a satin stitch (such as for appliquéing or monogramming) or any satin-stitch shapes (such as filled-in scallops, flowers, leaves, hearts, and so on), the fabric won't feed and then the machine jams. What is wrong?

The most likely causes for this problem are using the wrong thread, the wrong presser foot, or the wrong stitch length.

Try a finer thread, such as cotton machine-embroidery thread size 50 or finer (higher number). Switch to a satin-stitch foot, which has a groove on the underside to allow the build-up of thread to pass underneath without being crushed. Finally, try a longer stitch length. If the stitch length is too short, the stitch will be too dense and the thread will build up, resulting in a jam.

Also, be sure the machine is clean, especially the bobbin area. Use a tear-away stabilizer under the fabric. Use a new, good-quality needle of the appropriate size and type. (With medium-weight woven fabric, use size 50/2 or 60/2 cotton thread and a size 80 Universal needle.) Slightly loosen upper tension (adjust tension mechanism toward a lower number).

What does "mercerized" mean on cotton thread spool labels?

Mercerized thread has gone through a finishing process using a caustic-soda bath, which adds strength, luster, and dye affinity.

What is the difference between denim or jeans needles and Sharp sewing-machine needles? What are their uses?

Denim, jeans, and Sharp needles are all the same. All Sharp needles are designed to penetrate densely woven fabrics more easily than Universal needles. Until a few years ago, Sharp needles were readily available only in the large sizes—90/14, 100/16, and 110/18, and were called denim or jeans needles because that was their primary use. Now Sharps are available in smaller sizes, including 70/10 and 80/12. Schmetz has also added Microtex/Sharp needles in sizes 60/8 to 90/14; these are Sharps with a slimmer design for very fine, tightly woven, silky fabrics such as microfibers.

Universal needles, used most often, have a slightly rounded point, which deflects off fibers rather than piercing them. This deflection can occasionally make some stitches appear crooked, but there are very few instances when this would be noticeable. Universal needles work well on most wovens or knits.

Sharp-type needles actually pierce fibers. For this reason, they are not recommended for knits, where piercing the fibers would cause holes. They penetrate densely woven fabrics better than Universals, but are also sometimes used when a perfect stitch is desired, for example, for topstitching.

Should a straight-stitch needle plate be used whenever a straight-stitch foot is used?

Not necessarily. A straight-stitch needle plate has only a round hole opening for the needle and offers extra support underneath the fabric, the same way a straight-stitch foot does on top of the fabric. It prevents the fabric from being pushed into the bobbin area. If you are experiencing that problem, first try a new, good-quality needle. Be sure it is the right size and type for the fabric and thread. If you must start stitching at the very edge of a soft, lightweight fabric, put the corner of a piece of lightweight stabilizer underneath and slightly pull the thread tails to get started. For a temporary straight-stitch plate, cover the oval needle opening of a standard needle plate with tape.

Straight-stitch needle plates are usually expensive. But if much of your sewing consists of straight stitching on soft, lightweight fabrics and you have persistent problems doing so, then a straight-stitch needle plate might be worth a try.

My friend has the same brand and model machine that I do, yet the upper tension on my machine consistently needs to be set to a lower number than on hers. Is there something wrong with my machine?

Probably not. It is not at all unusual for tension settings to vary among individual machines. This is not a concern unless you have to go nearly to zero ("0") for regular sewing. If this is the case (assuming your machine is clean and all other factors are correct), I would recommend asking your dealer to adjust your machine. Take along some pieces of the fabrics you sew most; otherwise stiff demo cloth might be used to test sew when setting the machine.

Should I adjust bobbin tension?

Once properly set for the thread you use most, bobbin tension should rarely be adjusted. Apparent bobbin-tension problems can be caused by lint caught in the bobbin tension device or by improper bobbin threading.

If your machine has a separate bobbin case, you can test bobbin tension by holding the thread and letting the case dangle. When you give the thread a jerk, the case should slip down. Occasional adjustments can be made by turning the adjusting screw to the right to tighten, or to the left to loosen it. Adjust the screw over a small box or a piece of fabric—the screw is tiny and easy to lose.

Some very attractive decorative effects can be created by sewing with the right side of the fabric down and with heavier threads (such as pearl cotton or ribbon thread) on the bobbin. Always bypass the bobbin tension device or loosen tension when using these heavier threads in the bobbin. Check your machine manual to see whether bobbin tension can be bypassed. If it cannot, you can loosen and later reset the bobbin tension on your regular bobbin case, but doing so repeatedly can be tedious. If you plan to use this technique often, you may want to invest in a separate bobbin case. If you do, mark the case to distinguish it.

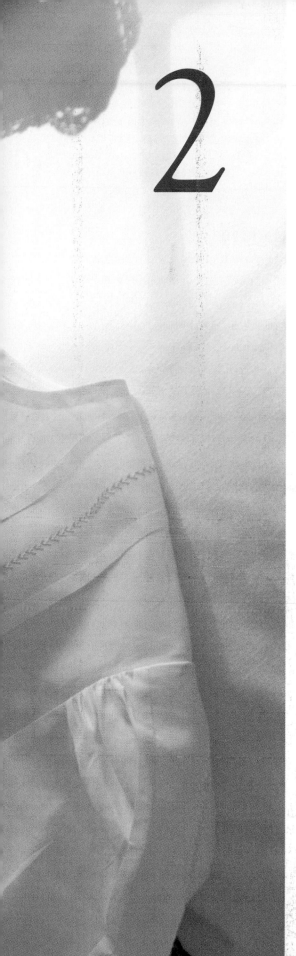

2 *Easy Ways to Achieve Precision in Your Sewing*

The look of delicate hand embroidery graces this white batiste blouse. Single-needle scallops frame briar-stitch fagoting and provide an attractive way to finish the raw edges underneath. Rows of folded tucks and feather stitching highlight the central motif. On the sleeve, tucks frame the fagoting as well as hiding the raw edges within. Pattern adapted from Harbor Blouse, Creative Needle *magazine, Sept./Oct. 1987.*

I am frequently asked how I achieve such even seam allowances, tucks, topstitching, and decorative stitching in my sewing. Accurate stitching is important not only for the look of the finished project, but also for proper fit. Most sewers realize this, but many think precision requires more time and effort than they have to spend on their sewing. In fact, much of what is needed is just "know-how." Some of the suggestions in this chapter may seem at first like extra work, but once you get used to them, they will actually save time, eliminate a lot of eyestrain and frustration, and make your sewing much more rewarding.

Cutting

Straighten the grain of your fabric. When a garment is cut off grain, the stitching can look "off" even if it was stitched correctly, especially once the garment has been washed.

For true crossgrain "cuts" on woven fabrics, clip through the selvage and tear the fabric whenever possible, instead of cutting. Tearing saves time and ensures accuracy. Always tear quickly; tearing slowly causes more pulls along the torn edge. On very delicate woven fabrics where tearing is risky, snip the fabric edge, pull a thread, and cut along the pulled thread.

When possible, do any decorative stitching on a piece of the fabric that is wider and longer than the pattern piece, then cut the pattern piece from the fabric. Since some stitching (for example, twin-needle pintucks) draws up the fabric, this sequence will ensure accurate fit. In addition, if you work this way, the very beginning and ending of the decorative stitching, where it is difficult to achieve perfect stitching, will be cut off.

For accurate measuring, cutting, straightening, and blocking, use cutting boards, rotary cutting boards, and pressing surfaces with horizontal, vertical, and diagonal lines marked. Gridded ironing-board covers eventually become distorted; they should be checked occasionally and replaced when necessary.

Marking

Mark stitch placement directly on the fabric only when you cannot use the fabric design (such as a stripe, plaid, or repeated design) or guides such as markings on a presser foot, needle plate, and so on instead. It is often possible to see the needle-plate edge or guidelines through the sheer fabrics commonly used for fine machine sewing. When marking is necessary, always test the fabric marker on a scrap of the fabric first, including carefully following instructions for removal. The marker must have a fine point for accuracy.

On delicate woven fabrics (such as handkerchief linen or Swiss batiste), mark the placement for a row of stitching that is too far from an edge or a previous row to use other guides by picking a thread at the fabric edge and pulling it enough to see it. You can press a crease along this line to make it more visible. (I usually have to pull a thread just once in a project, most often for the center-front stitch placement. I then plan the spacing for the other decorative stitching so that I can use guides, such as aligning the edge of the presser foot with a previous row of stitching.)

You can use crease lines for guiding whenever it's more convenient than marking or if you want to avoid excessive marking. For example, for a child's collar that called for a long length of 5-in. wide fabric to be stitched with 1/8-in. tucks every 1 in., I used crease lines instead of time-consuming marking, as shown in the photo at right. I chose a 5-in. wide eyelet with a 1-in. design repeat. (Eyelets fitting this criteria were not difficult to find.) Pressing crease lines at every design repeat was easy and eliminated marking.

Guides and guiding

The most accurate and even guiding is accomplished by using guides rather than by watching the needle. For most techniques, watch the needle only at the beginning of the stitching to determine the best guides to use. Then learn to watch only the guide, checking your stitching periodically and adjusting, if necessary. Not only will your stitching be more consistent, but your eyes will not tire as quickly.

Sit directly in front of the needle. Sewing-machine cabinets are designed so that the machine, rather than the needle, is centered in front of you. This machine position requires a person to lean left while sewing. This is not only less accurate for guiding, but also hard on your back. Most cabinet tops can be leveled (so that the machine sits at the level of the top of the cabinet, not in a well), and you can then reposition your machine so that the needle is directly in front of you.

If your machine has a removable table for creating a larger stitching surface, use it whenever you do not need the free arm. The larger surface allows more control for guiding and allows more space for adding guiding aids. If your machine does not have a large sewing surface, a generic table, available through sewing machine dealers or by mail order, may work.

NEEDLE POSITIONS

As discussed in Chapter 1, the machine will do the best job of feeding the fabric evenly when the presser foot holds the

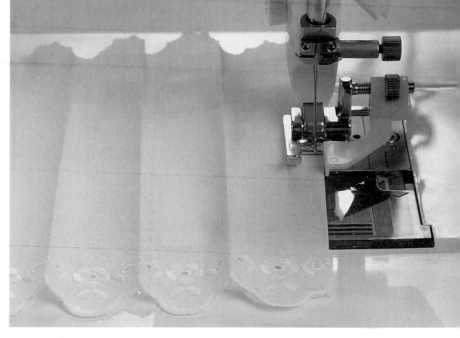

Pressing crease lines can be a time-saving alternative to measuring and marking. For a child's collar that called for tucks every 1 in., choosing an eyelet having a 1-in. design repeat made marking with crease lines easy. A blind-hem foot guides the stitching for accurate ⅛-in. tucks along each crease line.

fabric securely over both feed dogs. Changing needle positions allows you to use the best presser foot and fabric position for the job without compromising feed. For example, when sewing close to a fabric edge, rather than shifting the fabric edge close to the needle, move the needle instead so that the fabric stays over both feed dogs, as shown in the photo at right.

Generally, for seam allowances or tucks wider than about ½ in., guide the fabric edge along markings on the needle plate or other guide, and adjust the needle position, if necessary. For seam allowances or tucks between approximately ³⁄₁₆ in. and ½ in. wide, guide the edge of the fabric even with the right edge of the foot and move the needle to the best position for the correct spacing. Only when you are sewing closer than ³⁄₁₆ in. from an edge do you usually have to switch to a foot (such as an edging foot) that guides the fabric

To sew close to a fabric edge while keeping the fabric over both feed dogs, move the needle toward the fabric edge instead of moving the fabric edge to the needle.

METRIC CONVERSION CHART

U.S. MEASUREMENT	METRIC EQUIVALENT
1/16 in.	1.5mm
1/8 in.	3mm
3/16 in.	4.5mm
1/4 in.	6mm
3/8 in.	10mm (1cm)
1/2 in.	13mm (1.3cm)
5/8 in.	15mm (1.5cm)
1 in.	25mm (2.5cm)

TIPS

On many machines the needle position can be changed by selecting straight stitch, then using the width selector. If this moves the needle in only one direction, try engaging mirror image (if your machine has this feature) to move the needle in the other direction.

On some machines engaging the twin-needle option, whether or not you are using twin needles, may allow more needle positions.

over just one feed dog. (For metric conversion, see the chart above.)

Note that when using a straight-stitch foot, the needle must be in center position. (With any other needle position, the needle would hit the foot and break.) Ideally straight-stitch feet should cover as much of the feed dogs as possible, but some feet that have guidelines for sewing 1/8 in. and 1/4 in. from an edge actually cover the feed dogs very little. The flat underside and small needle-hole opening on these feet compensate to some extent because they hold the fabric extra well. However, feed-dog spacing varies, so experiment with these feet on your machine. The advantage of their readily apparent guides may outweigh the disadvantage of the fabric not being held by both feed dogs.

Most newer sewing machines allow the needle position to be changed. Some have only three needle positions, while others have almost unlimited positions. Some allow needle position to be changed with straight stitches only, others with most stitches. Consult your machine manual for information on needle positions.

PRESSER FEET

When choosing a foot for a stitching task, consider not only the foot's function, but also characteristics that can help with guiding, such as markings or notches on the foot, the foot's size, and so on (even its edges can be used as guides). Also bear in mind that presser feet with flat undersides are preferred for regular straight stitching, and those with indented undersides are best for satin stitching or other raised effects.

Presser feet can be used for purposes other than their name implies. For example, Bernina's jeans foot (#8) is a straight-stitch foot that can be used with other fabrics as well. Elna's blind-stitch foot has a long adjustable guide that makes it a perfect adjustable edging foot. The grooves of pintuck feet can be used as guides, for example, to guide corded fabric edges for fagoting (see p. 104).

Many straight-stitch feet are designed so that the edges of the feet, toes, grooves, or markings can be used as guides for precision straight stitching close to an edge. These feet may be called "quilter's," "patchwork," or "1/4-in. feet" (see the upper photo on the facing page).

You can use an extra-fine permanent marker to help identify presser feet, as well as to add markings to help with guiding. For example, some Pfaff feet have helpful guidelines on the clear section in the center of the foot, but the marks do not go all the way to the front of the foot where it meets the fabric. I put additional marks at the front edge. Elna's multiple-cord foot can be used either with or without cord as a metal embroidery foot, but I add a mark to the center front of the foot for guiding, as shown in the lower photo on the facing page. Marks can usually be removed with alcohol, but to be sure, test first in an inconspicuous place.

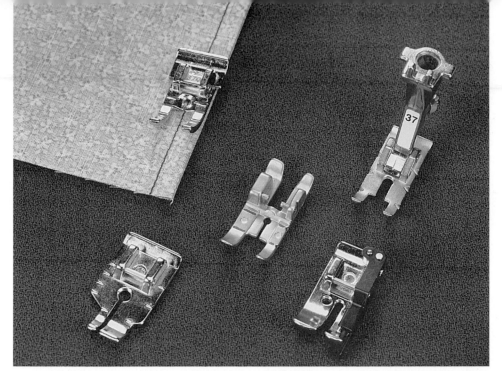

Presser feet can be used for purposes other than those implied by their names. So-called 'patchwork' and 'quilter's' feet are not just for quilters—they can be used as guides for any straight stitching ¼ in. or ⅛ in. from an edge.

NEEDLE PLATE

Use needle-plate guideline markings as well as the edge of the needle plate. Unfortunately, most needle-plate guidelines are marked for millimeters, while most instructions for seam allowances are in inches in this country. Millimeter guidelines can still be very helpful though, especially when used in combination with different needle positions.

Consult your sewing-machine manual for suggestions on guiding with particular feet, guides, or the needle plate. You may find such information in sections on needle positions, pintucks, tucks, pleats, topstitching, or edgestitching.

You can add helpful markings to your needle plate also. On some Bernina models, the needle plates have guidelines calibrated in inches, but not identified. I put an identifying mark at the front of the lines I use most (¼ in. and ⅝ in.).

On some New Home machines, the needle plates have inch guidelines toward the back. I put a corresponding line near the front of the needle plate for the distances I use most. (On New

You can mark your own guidelines directly on presser feet using an extra-fine permanent marker. A center mark was added on this Elna multiple-cord foot.

Home machines where the needle comes up automatically in the left needle position, the needle-plate guidelines measure from this position.)

SEAM GUIDES

There are seam guides that snap onto the needle plate or screw onto the machine bed for guiding an even distance from the fabric edge. These can be combined with different needle positions for narrower or wider spacing. For example, Elna has a snap-on "cloth guide" with a raised sliding guide that works very well for guiding 10mm to

Stitching circles and arcs

You can stitch perfect circles or sections of circles (such as large scallops) by using a bent pin taped to the bed of the machine as a pivot. Bend a pin in half and tape it, point up, to the right or left of the needle, as shown in the photo below left. The distance from the pin to the machine needle should be the radius of the circle. Stabilize the fabric well and impale it on the pin. Keep the center of the circle on the pin with a clean cork, eraser, or your fingers as you stitch (see the photo below right). (A thumbtack taped point up is often recommended for this technique. But even if the thumbtack is new, the point can damage many fabrics, so I don't recommend it.) Some Elnas have holes on their removable tables and a tack-like pivot for this technique. The table works great, but on more delicate fabrics, I recommend inserting a fine pin into the holes for the pivot.

To stitch perfect scallops or circles, tape a bent pin to the right or left of the needle (left). The distance from the pin to the needle will be the radius of the circle. An eraser stuck on the pin over the fabric helps control the fabric as it pivots (right).

75mm from an edge. It can be used with the 10mm line and far right needle position to stitch as close as ¼ in. to almost 3¼ in. with the 75mm line and far left needle position.

Other guides, sometimes called "Quilting Guides," slide into the needle bar behind the presser foot for even spacing from an edge or another row of stitching.

For stitching straight rows, long guides will give the best results. For curves, use just a point directly to the right or left of the needle as a guide. For stitching circles and arcs, see the sidebar at left.

Avoid any guides that are wobbly · and cannot be tightened. They are not accurate.

TAPE

Masking tape or drafting tape applied parallel to the presser foot on the machine bed may be used as a guide. You can create a raised guide by using several layers of tape. (Rubbing alcohol will usually remove any sticky residue that remains after you have removed the tape.) Even the sticky top edge of 3M's Post-it Notes can be used for a quick, temporary guide.

RUBBER BANDS

A medium to wide rubber band that fits securely around the machine free arm makes an easy temporary guide (see the upper photo on the facing page). If the machine has a removable table, you can create a longer guide by positioning a second rubber band around the front of the table so that it aligns with the one on the free arm.

CREATIVE GUIDES

In addition to these suggestions, be creative, and try anything you think may be helpful. For example, a flat coffee stirrer taped in front of the presser foot

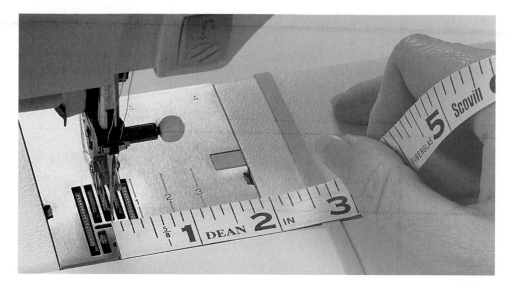

A rubber band placed around the free arm can serve as a guideline where there is none or extend a short guide. On this machine an additional rubber band on the front of the removable table further lengthens the guideline.

is great for maintaining an even space between two pieces of fabric for fagoting (see the photo on p. 103). Use stirrers of different widths to allow for wider or closer spacing between the two fabrics. Check for other guiding aids in catalogs and in notions displays at sewing-machine dealers and fabric stores.

TAKING MEASUREMENTS AND RECORDING THE RESULTS

I recommend measuring with an accurate flat ruler, seam gauge, or graph paper to determine the best foot, marking on the foot, needle plate and needle-position combination for the most common topstitching and seam allowances. Record the results on an index card (see the sidebar on p. 34) and keep it near your machine so that the information is always just a glance away.

Starting, ending, and securing the stitching

When possible, start slightly in from the edge of the fabric so that the fabric is securely under the presser foot, especially for stitching techniques that are

Putting the corner of the fabric over a piece of tearaway stabilizer and slightly pulling the thread tails as you begin to stitch help to start difficult stitching at the very edge of the fabric.

difficult to get started. The very beginning and end of the stitching will often be hidden in a seam or cut off anyway.

When you must start right at the fabric edge, slightly pull the thread tails to get started, as shown in the photo above right. It is often helpful to put the edge of the fabric over the corner of a small piece of tearaway stabilizer.

Creating your index-card reference

An index card for your most-used machine setups will be immensely useful, since you won't have to keep recreating them from scratch. Before taking measurements, though, make sure your needle is truly centered for a straight stitch in center needle position. If it's not, ask your machine dealer to adjust it.

Measuring with a flat ruler or seam gauge

To measure with a flat ruler or seam gauge, put the ruler on the bed of the machine beneath the needle. Manually lower the needle point to either the "0" or the 1-in. line, as

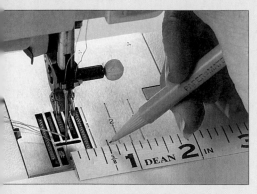

Aligning the '0' position of a tape measure with the needle point helps determine the best foot, guide, and needle position for common seam allowances. On this machine (Pfaff 7550), when the needle is set two positions left of center, the machine's 1.5cm line marks a perfect 5/8-in. seam allowance.

shown in the photo below left. Then experiment with feet, guides, and needle positions to determine the combinations that give you the topstitching and seam-allowance widths you use the most. (You can use a tape measure if you have checked its markings for accuracy.)

Measuring with graph paper

To use graph paper as a measuring tool, insert an old machine needle in the machine. (No thread is needed.) Align a line on the graph paper with a guide, such as a presser-foot edge, as shown in the photo at left above. Then straight-stitch about 1 in. with the needle in whatever position is closest to the desired spacing. On the graph paper note the guide used and the needle position. Repeat for other presser-foot guides and other presser feet.

To determine the best guiding combinations using guides on the machine bed, such as needle-plate markings, cut along a line on the graph paper. Use this cut edge to simulate a fabric edge, aligning it with the various guides and experimenting with different needle positions, as

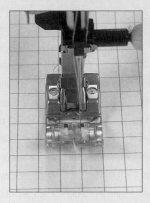 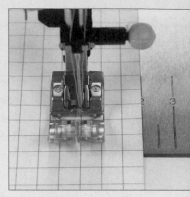

Graph paper makes it easy to evaluate guiding/needle position combinations. Aligning a line of the 1/4-in. graph paper with the edge of this presser foot (left) shows that with the needle set right of center, a perfect 1/4-in. seam allowance can be stitched. You can also cut along a graph-paper line and use that to simulate a fabric edge (right) to determine what guiding combination to use.

shown in the photo at right above. The graph paper makes it easy to see which combinations give the desired measurements. Discard the needle when you are finished.

Recording the results on your index card

Once you find the best combinations, test them on fabric, then note them on an index card. Keep it handy for reference.

Note that guiding can vary from person to person because using a guideline can mean aligning the fabric edge just at the line, on it, or over it. Find combinations that work for you and then be consistent, noting variances on your index card.

For example, here are my notes for the Elna Diva:

• 1/8 in.—Use left front edge of quilter's foot, or blind-stitch foot (E) with guide at center and far left needle position.

• 1/4 in.—Use right front edge of quilter's foot, or use 10mm needle-plate line and needle far right.

• 1/2 in.—Use 10mm line, needle far left.

• 5/8 in.—Use 15mm line, needle near left.

• 1 in.—Use right edge of needle plate, needle near right.

• 2 in.—Use edge of removable sewing table, needle center.

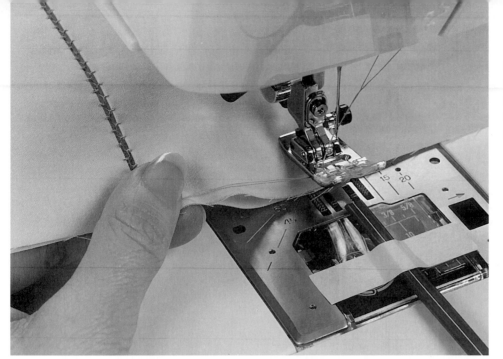

Pinching the threads as you pull the fabric away from the machine prevents the stitching at the fabric edge from distorting.

At the end of the stitching, gently pull the fabric out from under the presser foot, then pinch the threads at the end of the stitching as you continue to pull the fabric and threads away from the machine, as shown in the photo above. This prevents the fabric and stitching from being distorted, which often occurs when the threads are pulled too roughly at the end.

When it is necessary to secure straight stitching, the method to use depends on the weight of the fabric. On medium- to heavy-weight fabrics, backstitch to secure the stitching. Start the stitching with the needle about ⅜ in. in from the edge, stitch in reverse to the edge, then sew forward as usual.

Do not backstitch lightweight fabrics because doing so causes an unattractive puckered area. If securing is necessary, shorten stitch length to about 1mm for ⅜ in. at the beginning and end of the stitching. (It is helpful to pull the threads tails slightly at the start.) Another option is to tie the top and bobbin thread tails together on the underside or next to the fabric edge, then "bury" the tails.

To bury thread tails cut the tails long. Take the top thread to the underside and knot the top and bobbin threads together next to the fabric. Then thread both tails into the eye of a hand needle. Stitch into the seam allowance right next to the knot, then bring the needle out about ³⁄₁₆ in. away. Cut the threads close to the fabric, and the ends will disappear. Bury thread tails whenever they would show on the finished project, for example, at the end of topstitching.

When decorative stitching must be secured (for example, for individual flower motifs that do not tie off automatically), stitch in the same place several times. Most newer machines have a securing option or button for this. Or you can manually set the machine at "0" width and "0" length for several stitches.

TIP

Maintain accuracy and save time when stitching several small pieces that have the same seam allowance by sewing one immediately after the other, rather than starting and ending each one separately. As soon as you get to the end of one piece, start the next one, without raising the presser foot. Cut the pieces apart afterward.

Additional tips

Following are some additional tips for achieving accurate and precise stitching:

• Do not sew over pins. Remove them before they reach the presser foot. (Sewing over pins distorts stitching and risks damaging the needle.)

• Stitch with a smooth speed.

• Stop with the needle down when you need to adjust the fabric.

• In most cases, press after each step. Be careful not to stretch fabric or laces when pressing.

• Stitch test samples with exactly the same conditions (including grain direction, number of fabric layers, stabilizer, and so on) as on the project.

• Make notes, including guiding information, right on the fabric sample and save it in your notebook for future reference.

Applications

Anything that ensures accuracy will improve almost any sewing technique. Keep in mind that you are more likely to use the best foot, guide, and needle-position combinations you have worked out if the index card with your notes is always handy. Whenever you figure out other useful guiding information, add it to your card.

SEAMS

Accurate seam allowances are important for good fit. You can stitch precise seam allowances of any width if you use the appropriate guiding combination.

French seams (see the sidebar on the facing page) provide a professional-looking finish for very light- to medium-weight fabrics, especially sheer ones.

Most newer machines have several overlock-type stitches that are useful in certain seaming situations. The excess fabric is usually trimmed from the seam allowance after stitching. Consult your machine manual to see which ones you have and what their suggested uses are. Test for the best guiding combination to get a ⅝-in. (or other width) seam allowance. Add this to your index card, noting the stitch width since that will make a difference.

For example, on the Elna Diva the super overlock stitch (#9) is excellent for finished seams on light- to medium-weight fabrics where French seams are not appropriate. I often use this stitch to set in sleeves. The index card entry might read: "⅝-in. seam allowance with stitch width 4.4mm—use 15mm line, needle far right."

TUCKS AND PLEATS

Guiding combinations will help you stitch perfect folded tucks and pleats with very little marking. For more on making folded tucks , see the sidebar on p. 105 and pp. 123-124.

ROWS OF DECORATIVE STITCHING

Guiding aids enable you to stitch evenly spaced rows of decorative stitching, either an even distance from an edge or from another row, without marking. For example, using tape or a rubber band to guide the folded lower edge of a skirt will eliminate having to mark the stitching line for hemming from the right side with decorative stitches (see p. 63 and pp. 122-123).

French seams

For perfect French seams on medium-weight fabrics (such as broadcloth and most prints) with a ⅝-in. seam allowance, follow these steps, as shown in the photo below:

1. Stitch one ⅜-in. seam with wrong sides together.
2. Press both seam allowances first to one side then the other.
3. Trim the seam allowance to ⅛ in.
4. Fold right sides together and stitch a ¼-in. seam enclosing the trimmed seam allowances.

The ⅜-in. seam was sewn on a Pfaff 7550 using the right side of foot 0A, with two needle positions left. The ¼-in. seam was stitched at the same guiding, with five needle positions right.

Note that the width of both the first and second seam allowances of a French seam will vary according to the width of the seam allowance provided for in the pattern as well as the weight of the fabric. On a very light-weight fabric, such as Swiss batiste, a finished French seam should be no wider than ⅛ in. to 3/16 in.

With a good guiding reference French seams are easy.
1. With wrong sides together, stitch a ⅜-in. seam.
2. Press seam allowances to one side, then the other. Trim to ⅛ in.
3. Fold right sides together; stitch a ¼-in. seam, enclosing first seam.

TOPSTITCHING, EDGESTITCHING, AND UNDERSTITCHING

By taking advantage of the ability to move the needle left and right of center, you usually can topstitch, edgestitch, and understitch with the fabric edge aligned with the right edge of the presser foot and over both feed dogs (see the discussion of needle position on pp. 29-30). This avoids many of the problems typically encountered when trying to guide evenly with the fabric over just one feed dog.

For stitching even closer to the edge, try an edging foot or a straight-stitch foot with guides, such as a quilter's foot.

PIPING

For precise and consistent application of piping, use a presser foot with one or more grooves, such as a standard button-hole foot, to guide small piping. For stitching close to large piping, use a zipper foot. When making up the piping, set the needle to stitch one position away from right alongside the piping. Then when sewing the piping into the project, use the needle position closest to the piping. This prevents the common problem of having the first stitching visible.

GATHERING

Use a combination of guiding and needle position to make perfectly spaced rows of lengthened stitching for gathering a skirt, setting in a sleeve, and so on. For example, here is a way to gather any fabric where the needle will not leave holes (the seam allowance is ⅝ in.):
1. Loosen upper tension and stitch one row of lengthened stitches ¾ in. from the fabric edge.
2. Stitch a second row ⅜ in. to ½ in. from the edge.
3. Pull up the bobbin threads to the desired fullness.

4. To attach the gathered fabric, return the stitch length and upper tension to normal and stitch ⅝ in. from the edge, between the two gathering rows.
5. Remove the gathering stitches. (The loosened upper tension makes it easier to remove the bobbin threads before the top threads.)

A word about comfort

Aching backs and eyestrain are the bane of sewers everywhere (see the sidebar on the facing page). Take the time to assess your work area from an ergonomic point of view; a few minor adjustments could make a world of difference in your work as well as in your comfort.

Questions

How do you determine which fabric marker to use on a particular fabric?
Test fabric markers carefully on a scrap of the fabric. This takes some advance planning, but I have learned the hard way that not testing is risky. (Each pleat line marked with an air-erasable pen on a teal faille moiré—51% acetate, 49% cotton—skirt is now permanently discolored to a light blue. The water-erasable pen markings I thought had been carefully removed with cold water on a Swiss cotton piqué blouse kept reappearing whenever it was ironed, often leaving a brownish-colored residue.) Always mark a scrap of the fabric with any markers you are considering, then follow the removal method (usually rinsing) recommended on the package. Let the fabric dry, press it, and note the results. If you are testing a pencil mark, wash the fabric scrap as you intend to wash the completed project.

Write notes directly on the fabric scrap, such as "Italian organdy—not pre-washed; blue water-erasable marker

Preventing backache and eyestrain

To prevent backache, a high cutting table is essential. The best cutting-table height depends on your own height—just below hip height works well for me. Since my family rarely uses the table in our formal dining room, I have elevated it with several old books under each leg, and I use this for cutting fabric. If this is not an option for you, consider some of the very functional and reasonably priced cutting tables available at fabric stores and through sewing-machine dealers. For pinning and for cutting out small items, I use the ironing board adjusted to a comfortable height.

Setting up your sewing area

For machine sewing, invest in a rolling secretary's chair with adjustable height and backrest. Position the sewing machine so that the needle bar is directly in front of you (see p. 29). On many sewing- machine cabinets, the section on which the machine rests can be raised to be level with the rest of the cabinet, like a desk top, allowing you more leeway for positioning the machine. Also experiment with different foot-pedal positions.

The importance of guides

To prevent eyestrain, learn to use guides. Watch the needle only when absolutely necessary—usually just at the beginning of each technique. Once the settings and guiding position are determined, force yourself to watch only the fabric at the guide. Check your work occasionally and adjust your guiding, if necessary. Using a guide is easier on the eyes (and back, because you do not have to lean over as much), and is also much more accurate than watching the needle. Although it may take some practice, using a guide definitely works.

Lighting

Your sewing area should have good general room lighting as well as task lighting for machine and hand work. I use a halogen floor lamp to illuminate the room; for more direct light at the machine and for hand work, lamps with adjustable arms work well. They may be freestanding or clamp onto the cabinet or table. Just don't leave a very hot bulb right next to the machine for a long time; doing so could discolor or distort some machine cases.

Finally, take frequent breaks—at least long enough to stand up and stretch, and look off into the distance to rest your eyes.

reappeared twice when ironed; purple air-erasable marker caused no problems." Also note other variables, such as "pre-washed, spray starched, and pressed before marking."

Keep the fabric scraps and notes in a file, envelope or in a pocket page in your sample notebook, along with the package instructions for each marker. This is valuable for future reference so you will not have to test the same fabric again. Even with a successfully tested marker, it is wise to mark very sparingly.

Do you have any tips for sewing over thick seams, like those on jeans hems? My machine keeps stitching in one place and jams, and/or jumps off the thickness, leaving a space with no stitching.

First, eliminate as much bulk as possible. On jeans, I often serge or overcast the raw lower edges and then turn them up only once for stitching—the once-folded hem is easier to stitch and is a good option, unless for some reason, the underside will show or the wearer specifically wants the traditional double-fold jeans hem. With the right tools though, you can handle the thickness of even a traditional jeans hem.

Use a denim needle appropriate in size for the fabric (I use size 90 the most). The sharp point will help pierce the thick fabric. When the presser foot starts onto a thick seam and angles up, stop with the needle down, raise the presser foot, and put a shim under the back of the presser foot to make it level. The shim can be the plastic box for

sewing-machine needles; folded-up fabric, paper, or cardboard; or a notion that is specifically designed for this purpose. Lower the presser foot and continue stitching.

As you stitch off the thick seam, slightly lift the fabric behind the presser foot to allow the foot to roll off the thickness rather than jump off, skipping stitches. If the seam is exceptionally thick, a shim may be needed in front too. In this case, when the front of the presser foot goes off the thick seam, the foot angles down. Stop with the needle down, raise the presser foot and put a shim under the front of the foot (in front of the needle). When the back of the foot clears the thick seam, gradually pull the shim out toward the front as you stitch.

What is directional stitching?

Directional stitching refers to the practice of stitching in the same direction for like applications in order to avoid distortion of the fabric. For example, when applying a centered zipper, it's best to stitch each side across the lower edge and then up, rather than down one side, across, and up the other. In general seams should be stitched from top to bottom (though there are sewers who recommend stitching from the wide end toward the narrow end). In any case, after you have found what works best for you, the most important thing is to be consistent. If you stitch one side seam from top to bottom, stitch the other side seam from top to bottom as well. Fabrics with a nap should be stitched "with the nap" (the way the pile feels smooth when stroked). If there is any doubt about the best direction to stitch a fabric, do some test stitching on scraps.

I am having difficulty getting two rows of scallops to mirror and match each other exactly. What would cause this problem? Could stitching speed be a factor?

Yes, it is possible that speed could slightly affect stitch density. The difference would hardly be noticeable except when two rows of stitching must match exactly, as in the situation you describe.

I tested the effect of stitching speed by stitching three rows of ten baby scallops, each at a different speed. The row stitched at a medium speed (using the "slow" speed button) was 80.5mm long. The row stitched at a fast speed measured 82.5mm. The third row, which was stitched while varying the speed from slow to fast, was almost 83mm long.

For decorative stitching, the best results are obtained with a slow to medium speed and smooth, even stitching. For this reason, some of the newer machines automatically switch to a slower speed with this kind of stitching.

The problem you describe can have other causes. The stitching may be too dense. In this case use finer machine-embroidery thread (and an appropriate new needle) and lengthen the stitch slightly. Using the wrong presser foot can also cause uneven satin stitching; use a satin-stitch foot, which has a channel underneath to allow the stitching to pass under the foot easily. If the presser foot rides over part of the previous stitching, the stitching will be affected. Unfortunately, this sometimes cannot be avoided. Always stitch a sample and, if necessary, adjust the second row of stitches to match the first using the balancing feature (also called elongation or fine-tuning feature) or possibly the stitch-length adjustment. Any other difference between one row and the next, such as more or fewer layers of fabric, different grain direction, mirror-image stitching, or stitching in

the opposite direction, could also slightly affect the stitch and require adjustments when an exact match is required.

If the fabric is not adequately stabilized, the lengths of motifs can be affected. For decorative stitching, most fabrics should be prewashed and spray starched, and then stitched with a tear-away stabilizer underneath. (A lightweight stabilizer should be used under lightweight fabrics.) After stitching gently tear away the stabilizer.

Finally, a flat sewing surface will also help. If your machine has a sewing table, use it whenever the free arm is not needed.

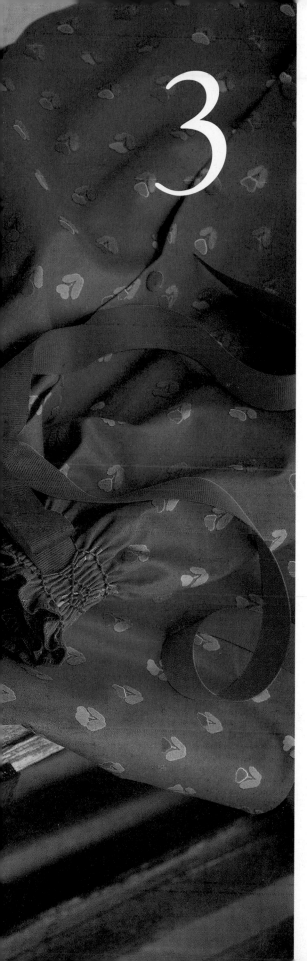

3 Decorative Edges and Creative Appliqué

The colors of this cheerful tulip print are repeated in the ribbons that decorate the collar. The stretch blind stitch embellishes the ribbons and appliqués them to the blouse at the same time. The ruffled edges of the sleeves and skirt are finished with a picot edging, using the same stretch blind stitch.

Pattern adapted from Children's Corner #81, designed by Carol Laflin Ahles.

43

I n garment sewing as well as sewing for home decorating, there are many edges that need to be finished. Consider these: the neck, armhole, and lower edges on slips, nightgowns, and baby garments; the edges of ruffles; many sleeve edges (especially on little girls' garments); tablecloth, placemat, and napkin edges; and for smockers, smocked sleeve edges and the ruffled edge on smocked skirts, pinafores, sundresses, or pockets. You can create outstanding decorative edges for these applications using variations of common utility and decorative stitches. The same stitches can also be used for creative appliquéing.

Decorative edges

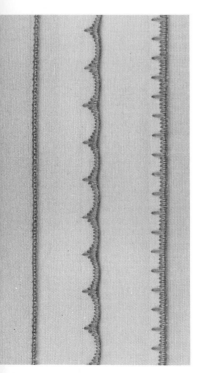

Three easy decorative edges are a corded edge (left), a 'no-trim-around' scalloped edge (center), and a picot edge (right).

When you want something more decorative than a plain, narrow-hem type finish, you can easily create a corded, scalloped, or picot edge using any of several common machine stitches. For these edge finishes (see the photo at left), the stitching is done on a folded edge, which makes it much more secure than stitching done on a raw edge. An additional advantage to stitching on a folded edge is that on the underside you simply trim away the excess fabric up to the stitching, rather than having to trim meticulously around the stitching on the right side, as is required with most other decorative edge techniques. (Eliminated is the tedious job of trimming around traditional scallops closely enough to eliminate whiskers without cutting the stitching itself!) And it's easy to add a touch of color by using contrasting thread.

The specifications that follow apply to corded, picot, and scalloped edges:

Fabric: Usually light- to medium-weight wovens.

Thread: Machine-embroidery cotton (DMC, Madeira, Mettler), usually size 50/2 or 60/2. Also experiment with other decorative threads as appropriate for the application, such as rayon or metallic thread for a Christmas tablecloth. Thread color can match or contrast with the fabric.

Needle: 70 or 80 Universal (or size and type appropriate for the fabric and thread). If fragile decorative threads are shredding with Universal needles, try Embroidery or Metallica needles from Schmetz or Metafil needles from Lammertz.

Upper tension: Loosen (decrease) slightly.

PREPARATION FOR CORDED, PICOT, AND SCALLOPED EDGES

To prepare for stitching any of the decorative edges, spray-starch and press under the raw edge about ½ in. (¼ in. on curves). If necessary on sharp curves, clip along the underside of the pressed-under edge.

If you are edging a ruffle on fabric that will be smocked (for example, for a smocked sleeve edge or smocked skirt, pinafore, or sundress), pleat the fabric for smocking first. Start the first row to be smocked the distance of the depth of the ruffle plus ½ in. from the edge. Leave long pleater threads. Press the pleated area flat, then press the raw edge under ½ in.

CORDED EDGE

The corded edge is the simplest of the decorative edges (just a zigzag stitch over cord along a fold), but it makes a very pretty edge. It is similar to the "roll and whip" (zigzag over a cut edge) technique from heirloom sewing, except that because you stitch over a cord and a fold, you end up with a stronger, more finished edge. This is also a very practi-

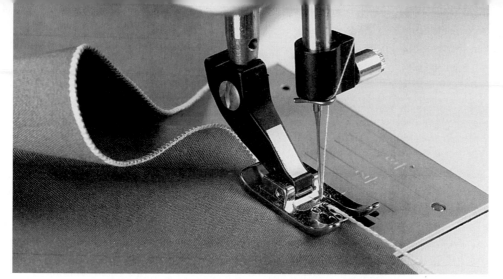

For the corded edge, a foot with holes or grooves helps keep the cord right next to the folded fabric edge. The stitch goes into the fabric on the left and just over the cord on the right.

cal way to finish fabric edges for fagoting—used with a pintuck foot, the corded edges make guiding especially easy (see p. 104).

If the excess fabric will be trimmed from the underside of the stitching (as is usually the case), this finish is not recommended for a loosely-woven fabric or for a garment that will get rough wearing and washing. Both the picot edge and the scalloped edge are sturdier, and therefore better choices, because of the wider zigzag in at least part of their stitch patterns.

Cord: Pearl cotton in size 5 for a heavier look, size 8 for a more delicate look. Other options for a delicate look include crochet cotton, buttonhole twist/topstitching thread, and so on. The cord size should be appropriate to the fabric and the look desired. Cord color should match thread color as closely as possible.

Foot: To guide the cord, a foot with one or more holes (like a cording foot or Bernina's embroidery foot with the hole in front) or grooves (like a buttonhole or pintuck foot) is helpful. On some machines and with certain stitches, the needle position can be moved so that you can use a foot with an off-center groove, such as a buttonhole foot, and adjust the stitch to align with the groove. Be creative. Sometimes even the curl of a narrow hemmer is very useful for guiding cord. If necessary, use a satin-stitch foot and hold the cord next to the fold with your hands.

Stitch: Zigzag.

Width: 2mm to 2.5mm (just wide enough for a secure "bite" into the folded fabric).

Length: About .8mm (a little longer than a satin stitch).

With the cord next to the folded edge of the fabric, stitch so that the left side of the stitch goes into the fabric and the right side goes just over the cord, as shown in the photo above. (The stitch must clear the cord, not go into it.) When using a foot with grooves, lifting the cord in front as you stitch helps to keep it in the groove. If you plan to trim the excess fabric up to the stitching on the underside, it is important that you make the stitch wide enough to be secure, but not so wide that it is unattractive. Adjust guiding and/or stitch width as necessary.

Zigzag stitch

For the picot edge, the even side of the stitch goes over and just off the folded edge. The side of the stitch that has the wide stitches goes into the fabric.
Using a strip of lightweight tearaway stabilizer underneath produces a more tailored look.

Stretch blind stitch

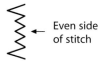

← Even side of stitch

Stretch stitch

← Even side of stitch

PICOT EDGE

The stretch blind stitch is usually recommended for blind hemming knits. However, if you shorten the stitch to the length you would use for a satin stitch, the stretch blind stitch makes a beautiful edging or appliqué stitch. (The shortened stitch is sometimes called a blanket stitch.) The wider stitches within the stitch pattern create a picot appearance. On stabilized fabric, the edging has a tailored look; on a lightweight, unstabilized fabric, it has a more delicate look, resembling baby scallops. (Note: Stitch numbers and settings for some machines are given on pp. 147-148.)

Foot: Satin stitch.
Stitch: Stretch (or elastic) blind stitch.
(On Berninas, use the stretch stitch; it takes two wide stitches rather than one.)
Width: 4mm to 5mm.

Length: about .5mm or less (as would be used for a satin stitch).
Stabilizer: Spray starching and pressing may be all that is needed for fabrics with body, especially if you want a delicate look. Otherwise, use a strip of lightweight, tearaway stabilizer underneath.

Stitch with the right side of the fabric facing up. Position the fabric so that the even or straight side of the stitch goes completely over and off the folded edge. Always test on a scrap of your fabric. If on your machine the even side of the stitch is on the right (as in the photo and drawings at left), the folded edge of the fabric will be to the right. (This is the case with most models of Elna, New Home, Pfaff, Viking, Kenmore.)

If on your machine the even side of the stitch is to the left and the stitch cannot be mirror imaged, the folded edge of the fabric must be to the left. (This is the case with the stretch stitch on models of Bernina that cannot mirror image.)

For a more delicate look, do not use stabilizer other than the basic spray starch and pressing; allow the widest zigzag in the stitch pattern to pull the fabric, creating a slight scallop effect. Sew taut, holding the fabric with your hands in front of and behind the presser foot. Adjust the stitch width and length, if necessary. If there is puckering, experiment with loosening upper tension a little more and/or applying more spray starch and pressing along the fold before stitching.

If you want the decorative edge to appear straighter and more tailored, stitch with a strip of lightweight tearaway stabilizer under the fold and extending at least ½ in. from the edge. You can use a shorter stitch length when you use a stabilizer. After stitching, gently tear away the stabilizer.

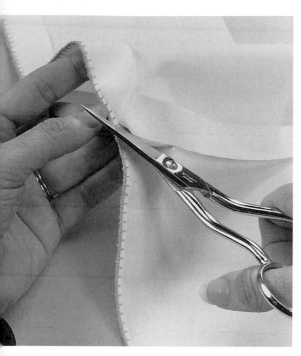

After stitching a decorative edge, trim excess fabric from the underside, just up to the widest stitches.

On the wrong side, trim away excess fabric, as shown in the photo above. Trim very close to the widest stitches using appliqué scissors or small scissors. The fabric will not ravel if it is trimmed closely and carefully. (Although it is possible to finish the raw edge of the fabric with overcasting or serging before pressing it under and stitching the decorative edging, this is really unnecessary.)

For some applications, you can narrow hem the edge before or possibly at the same time as you stitch the edging (see pp. 137-138).

Picot edging can be corded. The technique is the same as for the corded edge described earlier, except that the stretch blind stitch instead of the zigzag stitch is used. With the cord next to the folded edge, stitch so that the straight side of the stitch goes over the cord. A stabilizer may still be needed.

"NO-TRIM-AROUND" SCALLOPED EDGE

Many machines have an edging scallop —a variation of a scallop stitch—which makes a lovely shaped edging when you stitch it over a folded edge. When you use the edging scallop on the folded edge of a lightweight fabric, the wider zigzag stitches in the pattern actually pull in the fabric to create the scallops. The unique beauty of this version of scalloped edging is that you do not have to trim around every scallop on the right side; you need only trim up to the stitching on the underside. As with corded and picot edging, stitching over a fold creates a stronger, more finished edge.

The size of the scallop varies from machine to machine—from a tiny baby scallop suitable for children's garments or lingerie to a very large scallop suitable for bed linens. Some machines allow you to adjust the length of the scallop without altering stitch density. Even if your machine does not have this feature, using a slightly finer or thicker thread provides a little flexibility in the size of the scallop. For example, using a finer thread will allow you to shorten the scallop for a particular application, such as a baby garment. If the scallop is still too large or if your machine does not have the edging-scallop stitch, use the stretch blind stitch. As shown in the samples in the photo at right, on an unstabilized lightweight fabric the stretch blind stitch creates an effect very similar to a baby edging scallop.

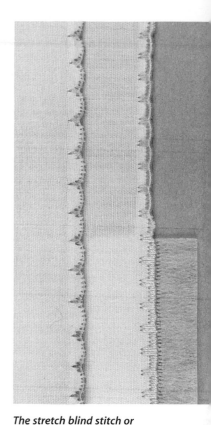

The stretch blind stitch or Bernina's stretch stitch can create a delicate scalloped effect similar to baby edging scallop (left) when stitched over a light- to medium-weight fabric without stabilizer (upper portion at right). When a stabilizer is used (lower portion at right), the straighter and more tailored look of picot edging is created.

Specifications are the same as for the picot edge with the stretch blind stitch (see p. 46) except for the following:

Fabric: For the baby edging scallop, additional suitable fabrics include tulle, tricot, and some knits.

Stitch: Edging scallop. If necessary, use the mirror-image function, so that the straight side of the stitch is to the right and the curved side is to the left, as illustrated.

Stabilizer: To form the scallop, the wide zigzag must be able to pull the fabric, so spray starching and pressing usually provide adequate stability. Occasionally on larger scallops, a very lightweight tearaway stabilizer is helpful. If the stabilizer is too stiff, the edging will be decorative, but it will not be pulled into scallops.

Stitch with the right side up and the folded fabric edge to the right, as shown in the photo below. Position the fabric so that the even or straight side of the stitch goes totally over and off the folded edge.

Edging scallop

The edging scallop stitch is used for 'no-trim-around' scallops. Hold the fabric taut with your hands in front of and behind the presser foot.

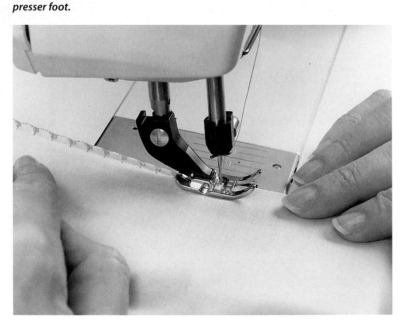

Hold the fabric taut with your hands in front of and behind the presser foot. If there is puckering, experiment with loosening upper tension a little more and/or more spray starching and pressing before stitching.

Trim away the excess fabric on the wrong side after stitching. Trim very close to the widest stitches using appliqué scissors or small scissors. The fabric will not ravel if trimmed very closely and carefully.

Note that this edge can also be narrow hemmed in advance or possibly at the same time as the edging is stitched (see pp. 137-138).

This stitch can be corded also. The cord lies alongside the folded edge, and the straight side of the stitch passes over the cord. The technique is the same as for the corded edge (see p. 44-45), except for the stitch used and possibly the presser foot: Since the cording will have to curve with the shape of the scallop, a foot with straight, narrow grooves, like a pintuck foot, may keep the cord too straight. If so, use one of the other feet suggested for cording or use a satin-stitch foot.

Creative appliqué

You needn't limit yourself to the traditional satin stitch for appliquéing! Attaching appliqués is an area where you can easily and effectively use your creativity to experiment with other machine stitches. For example, the same shortened stretch blind stitch used for the picot edge also makes a very pretty and different appliqué stitch(see the color photo on the facing page). As with the edging, the wide stitches in the pattern create a picot effect. (When I use this stitch to attach grosgrain ribbon to square collars, I am frequently asked where I found that wonderful grosgrain ribbon with picots!)

Dense, satin-type stitches, such as the shortened stretch blind stitch and the edging scallop (used for the "no-trim-around" scalloped edge) can be used for most appliqué projects, including those where raw edges must be covered. Open or running-type stitches, such as the feather stitch and the Parisian hem-stitch, are more appropriate for attaching appliqués with finished edges, such as ribbon, trims, purchased medallions, and faced or folded-edge appliqués (like those used for Madeira appliqué). The photo above right shows several stitches suitable for appliqué work.

Fabric: Most weights of cotton or cotton-blend wovens are traditional for appliquéing, but in fact very few fabrics should be rejected without at least being tested. With adaptations in thread, needle, settings, tension, stabilizer, and so on, almost any fabric appropriate for the project, including knits, ribbons and trims, lace, felt, lamé, and Ultrasuede, can be considered. If the finished project will be washed, also prewash the backing and appliqué fabrics if any of them could shrink or bleed. Prewashing to remove the sizing also makes many fabrics easier to stitch. Soft, stretchy fabrics may need a fusible interfacing to make them manageable.

Thread: Machine-embroidery cotton or rayon. Experiment with other decorative threads, such as metallics, as appropriate for the application. The size of the thread should be appropriate for the fabric; 50/2 or 60/2 cotton (40 in rayon) is usual for light- to medium-weight fabrics; 30/2 cotton (also 30 in rayon) for heavier fabrics. Thread color can match or contrast with the fabric.

For the bobbin thread you can use a fine thread (usually cotton) in white or a color to match the background fabric when decorative threads are used on the top. This saves the time and expense of

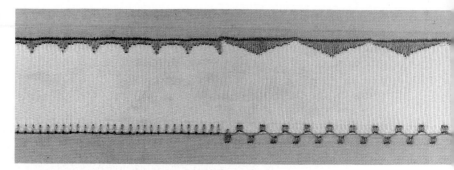

Many machine stitches are effective for appliquéing. Satin-type, dense stitches (top row) can be used on raw as well as finished edges; open or running-type stitches (bottom row) should be used only on folded or finished edges.

A purchased T-shirt becomes part of an eye-catching ensemble. A strip of fashion fabric to match the skirt has been appliquéd to the center of a ribbon and to the pocket at the same time using the stretch blind stitch.

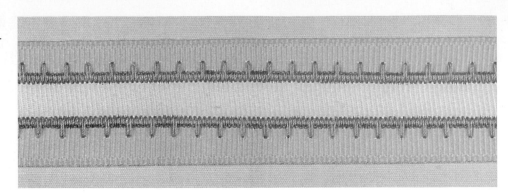

For this double ribbon trim, the edges of the narrow ribbon were appliquéd with the stretch blind stitch, securing both it and the wider grosgrain ribbon to the background fabric at the same time.

T I P

Fusible-web products are great for holding cut-out appliqués, but for holding ribbon and appliqués with finished edges, try fabric glue stick. Apply the glue to the back of the ribbon (or appliqué), being careful not to stretch the ribbon. Position the ribbon on the fabric, and let it dry a few minutes before stitching. The ribbons in the photo above were held in place with glue stick, then stitched.

changing the bobbin every time the top thread color is changed.

Needle: 70 or 80 Universal (or needle appropriate for the fabric and thread). If fragile decorative threads are shredding with Universal needles, try Embroidery or Metallica needles from Schmetz or Metafil needles from Lammertz.

Foot: For dense stitching, use a satin-stitch foot. For more visibility during stitching, you can use an open-toe satin-stitch foot. With open-toe feet it is critical that the fabric be well stabilized and/or in a hoop. For more open, running-type stitching, the indented area of satin-stitch feet is usually unnecessary; use the basic metal zigzag foot to hold the fabric more securely.

Stitch: Consider the following factors when choosing stitches for appliquéing:

• Finished edges (like those on ribbon or faced appliqués) will not ravel, so they do not have to be completely covered with stitching.

• Stitches should cover raw edges. Relatively dense stitches with a width of 2mm or more and a length of .5mm or less should generally be used.

• Some stitches that work beautifully on straight edges become distorted on curves. Therefore, the shape of your appliqué also determines stitch choices.

Width: Varies with application, but usually 3mm to 5mm. Small appliqués with detailed shapes are more attractive and easier to stitch with a narrower width (2mm to 3mm).

Length: Varies with stitch and application, but usually .5mm or less for satin-type stitches. Don't make the stitching too dense on lightweight fabrics.

Upper tension: Loosen (decrease) slightly. (Some Bernina models have the option of threading the bobbin thread through the hole in the finger of the bobbin case, which increases bobbin tension and creates more pull to the underside.)

Stabilizer: To prevent puckering and tunneling, a stabilizer is needed with any dense stitching, including most appliquéing. Use a tearaway stabilizer, appropriate in weight for the fabric, under the backing fabric. When more stability is needed, I prefer to use multiple layers of a lightweight tearaway rather than a single layer of a very heavy one. After the stitching is complete, gently tear off the stabilizer.

Prewash, spray-starch, and press the fabric, if appropriate for the fabric. Fuse or pin (with a few pins on the right side) a piece of lightweight stabilizer to the wrong side of the fabric. Then position the appliqué. As always, stitch a test sample and make any necessary adjustments before stitching your project.

Experiment with both utility and decorative stitches, keeping in mind the stitch specifications above. With some stitches, mirror imaging or stitching from the opposite direction will produce a completely different look. For example, when appliquéing with the shortened stretch blind stitch, the look is different depending on whether the wider stitches within the pattern go into the fabric or the appliqué, as you can see in the photo at right. Also experiment with matching as well as contrasting thread.

CORDING

Many appliqué stitches can be corded as they are stitched to give them more dimension. For the cord use pearl cotton, crochet thread, buttonhole twist/topstitching thread, and so on. The cord size should be appropriate for the fabric and the look desired. The color of the cord should match thread color as closely as possible.

A foot with one or more holes (such as a cording foot or Bernina's embroidery foot with the hole in front) to guide the cord is helpful. Feet with narrow, long, straight grooves (like some pintuck feet) work well if the appliqué shape does not require sharp curving. Test on scraps. If necessary, use a satin-stitch foot and hold the cord in place with your hands.

Questions

When I try to cord stretch-blind-stitch picot edging, the cord won't stay at the edge of the folded fabric. Can you help?
On some machines, it is difficult to keep the cord right next to the fabric edge—it rolls over or under the fabric. If the cord consistently and evenly rolls over

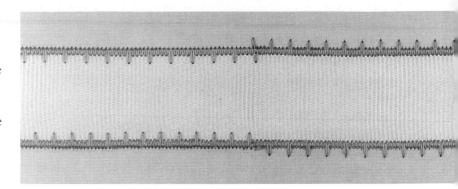

Changing the direction of a stitch can change the look of the appliqué. For example, this stretch blind stitch looks different when the picot is on the ribbon (left) and when it's on the background fabric (right).

the fabric and you like the look, that's fine. However, if you want it to stay alongside the folded edge, try any foot you have with one or more holes or grooves to guide the cord. If none of these works, try a satin-stitch foot and firmly hold the cord next to the fold with your hands. If the problem persists, do not use the cord. The effect of this edging is pleasing, uncorded as well as corded.

I use glue stick to hold fabrics in place for stitching. Is there any reason to use fabric glue stick rather than multi-purpose glue sticks from an office supply?
To answer your question, I compared several kinds of multi-purpose glue stick and fabric glue stick by testing them on the fabrics I use most. I got excellent results with all of them.

Just be sure the label lists fabric as one of the suggested uses and says that the glue is either water soluble or washes out. I would be cautious about using glue stick on an unwashable project that I planned to keep indefinitely because of possible unknown long-term effects such as discoloration.

One of my favorite uses for glue stick is to hold buttons in place for sewing either by hand or machine. However, before using any product on a special garment or project, it is always best to test it on that particular fabric.

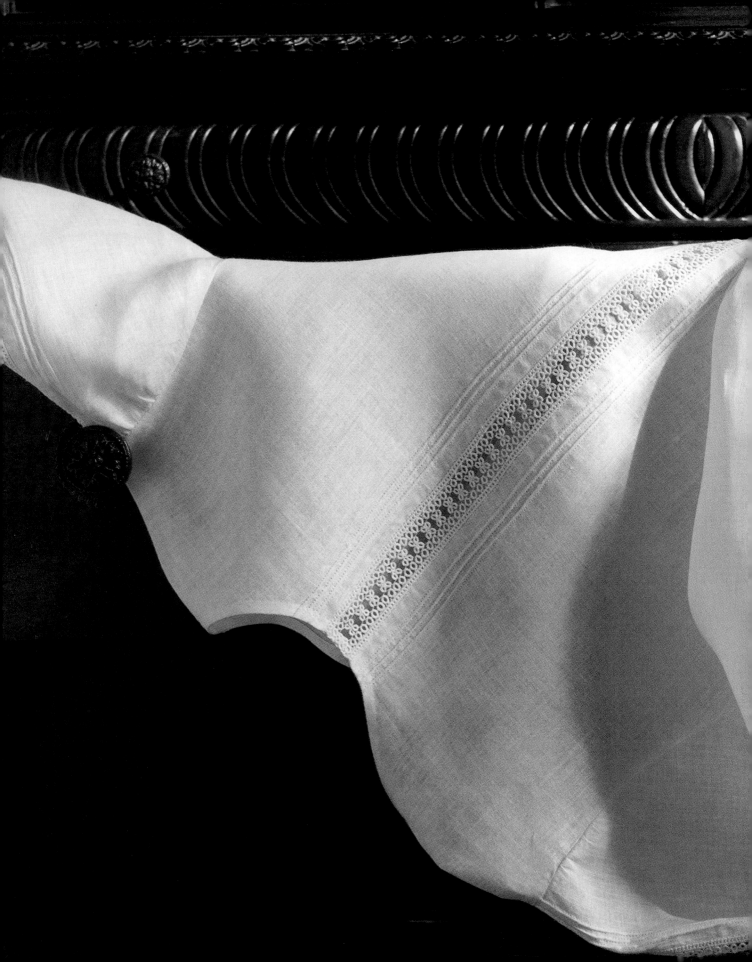

4 Twin-Needle Stitching

Delicate tatted insertion on this handkerchief linen blouse is highlighted with twin-needle corded pin-tucks. The tatting is sewn to the linen with a Venetian hemstitch, then the linen underneath is trimmed away. The motif is repeated on each of the sleeves.

S titching with twin needles opens many practical as well as creative possibilities. Twin needles allow you to:
• stitch two perfectly even rows of topstitching or decorative stitching at the same time;
• stitch both sides of a narrow ribbon or trim at the same time;
• add texture and/or color, especially when the stitching is corded;
• creatively hem a garment or disguise the crease line when letting down a hem (see the photo below);
• create pintucks on light- to medium-weight fabrics for a classic heirloom look;
• embellish sheer fabrics with a shadow-work effect.

Stitching with twin needles is easy. But to get the best results and the effects you want, it is important to know something about the needles themselves.

One use for twin needles is decorative hemming. This sample shows how three rows of corded twin-needle straight stitching can both stitch and embellish the top edge of a hem.

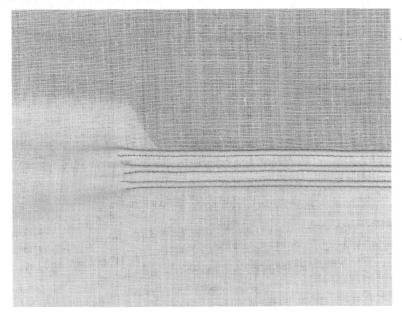

Twin needles

Twin needles (sometimes called double needles) will work in most zigzag sewing machines, except for those with a side-loading bobbin. Some machines require special twin needles. The requirements can vary not only by machine brand, but also by model within a brand. Twin needles can be distinguished by the color of their connecting bar near the top. The Schmetz twin needles that fit the greatest number of machines have a red bar. Needles for mechanical Elnas prior to the 7000 have a maroon bar, and those for unmodified Elna 7000's have a black bar, to give two other examples. (The needles angle differently for the best alignment.) If your machine came with twin needles, record the color of the bar and any identifying markings in your manual. To find out which twin needles should be used in your machine, check your machine manual, ask your dealer, or if necessary, perform the simple test described in the sidebar on the facing page.

TWIN-NEEDLE SIZE
Twin needles are labeled with two numbers separated by a slash. The first number is the distance between the two needles in millimeters; the second is the size of the needles. For example, 2.0/80 means size 80 needles, 2 millimeters apart. Twin needles that are relatively close typically have finer needles for use on lightweight fabrics, and those spaced farther apart have larger needles for heavier fabrics (see the photo on the facing page). Accordingly:
• needles spaced 1.6mm to 2mm apart are for decorative stitching or pintucks on lightweight fabrics;

• needles 2.5mm to 3mm apart are for decorative stitching or a pintuck/texturing effect on medium-weight fabrics;
• needles 4mm apart or more are for topstitching on medium- to heavy-weight fabrics.

SPECIALTY NEEDLES

Specialty needles such as stretch, jeans, and embroidery twin needles are also available for use on certain fabrics or with fragile decorative threads. Try these if the standard universal-point twin needles do not give satisfactory results.

Triple needles are also available. They have three needles joined to one bar and shank. (For the third thread you can wind an empty bobbin with the same thread and place the bobbin under one of the thread spools.) Like twin needles, triple needles can be used for topstitching, hemming, and decorative stitching with various machine stitches, but they do not really give the look of traditional pintucks.

Double wing needles have one Universal needle and one needle with wide metal "wings." They are used for a method of hemstitching (see pp. 70-71).

General specifications for twin-needle stitching are as follows:

Fabric: Light- to medium-weight wovens for pintucks; most weights of wovens or knits for decorative stitching, topstitching, texturing, and hemming.

Twin-needle stitching that creates a raised effect (such as pintucks or texturing) draws up fabric. For areas where garment fit could be affected, stitch on an oversized piece of fabric, then cut out the pattern piece(s).

Needle test

Whenever you are in doubt about using a needle in your machine, do the following test:
• With the machine set on straight stitch, turn the flywheel toward you to lower the needle and raise it again. Watch and listen for any indication that the needle is hitting or grazing anything, and if it is, do not use it.
• Next run the machine at a slow speed. If you hear a clicking sound, the needle is hitting something (usually the needle plate or the bobbin hook) and should not be used.
• If a wider stitch is desired, increase stitch width cautiously so that the needles will not hit the foot, needle plate, or bobbin hook as they cycle all the way to the right and left. If you hear clicking, narrow the width.

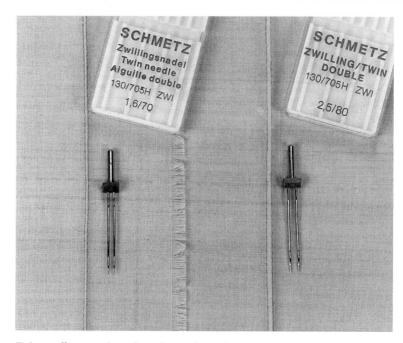

Twin needles come in various sizes and spacings. In general, the closer the two needles, the finer they are. The twin needles on the left are size 70, and the two needles are spaced 1.6mm apart; these would be used for pintucks on lightweight fabric. The heavier, more widely spaced needles on the right are for medium-weight fabric.

The hem of this delicate organdy pinafore is adorned with twin-needle corded pintucks, shadow-work scallops, and folded tucks embellished with the feather stitch. Fagoting is an additional detail added to the bib.

Always stitch a test sample with the same grain direction as on the project. Lengthwise stitching (parallel to the selvage) on some wovens is more likely than crossgrain stitching to pucker.

Thread: Machine-embroidery cotton, rayon, or other decorative threads for decorative stitching; fine machine-embroidery cotton or extra-fine cotton-covered polyester for pintucks; polyester, cotton-covered polyester, or other appropriate thread with strength and stretch to hem knits.

Thread size should be appropriate for the fabric. For example, use fine thread for a fine fabric. Thread color may match or contrast with the fabric. For

decorative stitching, you can also use a different color in each needle.

Cord: Pearl cotton, crochet thread, buttonhole twist/topstitching thread, and so on in a size appropriate for the fabric, the look desired, and the space between the two needles. The cord may match the fabric in color, or for a shadow effect on sheers, may contrast with the fabric.

Cording twin-needle stitching adds dimension and stability. (The cording is underneath the fabric, caught in the zigzag formed by the bobbin thread.) The method for cording twin-needle stitching is explained on pp. 59-60.

Foot: Pintuck foot, zigzag foot, satin-stitch foot. Use a pintuck foot for stitching pintucks or straight rows of texturing. (If more than one pintuck foot is available for your machine, generally choose one with narrower grooves for pintucking on lightweight fabrics with closely spaced twin needles, and one with wider grooves for texturing with the more widely spaced twin needles.)

Use a basic metal zigzag foot for less dense stitching when you want the fabric to stay flat.

Use a satin-stitch foot for dense stitching, to encourage a raised effect other than straight rows, or when a pintuck-type foot is unavailable for straight rows.

Width: When using any stitch other than a straight stitch with twin or triple needles, test the stitch width very carefully to avoid having the needles hit the presser foot and break. Test by stitching slowly through the stitch pattern. When approaching the farthest right side of the pattern, turn the flywheel by hand to be sure the needles clear the foot. Also test all the way to the left since many patterns are not centered as stitched.

To help prevent twin-needle break-age, some machines have a "twin-needle button" or option to limit the stitching width. This feature works differently on different machines. On some the stitch width is cut in half, on some it is narrowed by 2mm, and on some you can select the amount the width should be narrowed, based on the twin needles you are using. When using twin needles and stitch patterns with a width, such as scallops, it is prudent to test the width carefully even when using this option. If this feature limits the width too much (for example, if it limits width to the point that only very shallow scallops can be stitched), then disengage it, but test the width very carefully yourself.

Upper tension: Increase upper tension (adjust to a higher number) to create more of a raised effect. Loosen upper tension (adjust to a lower number) to keep the fabric flat or to reduce puckering. (Most necessary adjustments can be made with upper tension alone, but loosening or bypassing bobbin tension will also keep uncorded twin-needle stitching flat.)

Stabilizer: A stabilizer (other than spray starching and pressing) usually is not used for pintucks or texturing because it would keep the fabric flat, or for shadow work because it would be caught in the stitching and show through the sheer fabric. Unless the area is interfaced (as are collars, cuffs, lapels, and so on), a lightweight stabilizer may be needed to keep other twin-needle stitching flat, especially lengthwise stitching on wovens.

Threading: Check your sewing-machine manual for a diagram or instructions on threading for twin-needle stitching. Arrange the spools to avoid having the two threads rub together. (With two vertical spool pins, the thread should come off the back of

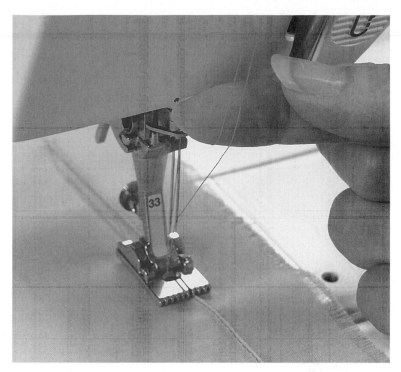

When using twin needles, make sure that the two threads are not twisted, especially directly over the needles.

one spool and the front of the other.) Usually the two threads are separated at the tension disc and over the needles. It is important that the two threads not be twisted together, especially directly over the needles (see the photo above).

Twin-needle pintucks

Twin-needle pintucks add a classic heirloom look to bodices, yokes, skirts, and sleeves, as well as to table or bed linens and home decorating items. Since they have a tailored look they are appropriate when other heirloom embellishments would be too frilly, for example on women's or older girls' garments, and on little boys' dress shirts. Pintucks alone can make a plain garment extraordinary.

You can experiment with different designs for stitching pintucks, such as stitching them in groups of three or more rows, stitching crossed rows for a waffle or diamond effect, or stitching shapes. Twin-needle pintucks are also an easy, attractive way to re-hem and hide the crease line at the same time when you are letting hems down. (It's best to make several rows of tucks, one of which is over the crease.)

Fabric: Light- to medium-weight wovens. Always stitch a test sample on a scrap of the fabric with the grain direction the same as on the project (see pp. 60-61).

Thread: Fine machine-embroidery cotton, such as Mettler 60/2, Madeira or DMC 50/2, or J. & P. Coats Dual Duty Plus Extra Fine. Color may match or contrast with the fabric.

Needle: Twin needles 1.6mm, 2mm, or 2.5mm apart with size 70 or 80 needles as appropriate for the fabric and thread. Ideally, the finer the fabric, the closer the needles and the smaller the needle size, for example, 1.6/70 for Swiss batiste.

Foot: A pintuck foot with multiple grooves on its underside will help make the tucks raised and equidistant. (If your machine has several pintuck feet available, the one with seven grooves is a good choice for most pintucks.)

If you do not have a pintuck foot and your machine has changeable needle positions, try a traditional buttonhole foot (or similar foot with grooves) and move the needles to align with one of the grooves, making sure the needles will not hit the foot. Otherwise, use a satin-stitch foot.

Stitch: Straight.

Length: About 2mm.

Upper tension: Normal to slightly loosened. Test.

MARKING AND MEASURING

It is usually necessary to use a wide guide or to measure and mark (pull a thread, press a crease, and so on) for only the first pintuck. For subsequent pintucks on the project, you can guide the first pintuck into another groove of the pintuck foot or alongside the foot to keep the

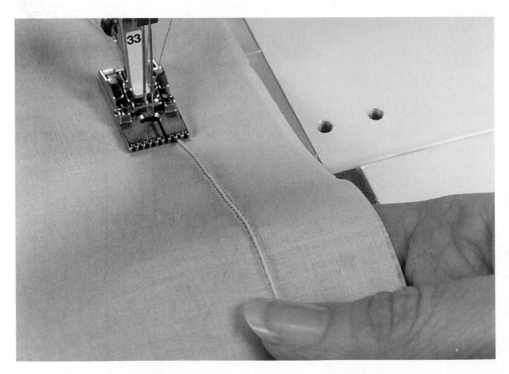

The best way to maintain even spacing with pintucks is to guide an adjacent, already stitched pintuck into another groove of the pintuck foot. Slightly lifting the fabric helps keep the pintuck in the groove.

spacing even between tucks, as shown in the photo on the facing page. Slightly lifting the fabric will help keep the pin-tuck in the groove.

CORDING

Cording pintucks can be a real problem solver. On stiff fabrics, such as organdy, it is difficult to get raised pintucks with-out tightening tension almost to the point of perforating the fabric along the stitching. Simply cording the pintucks and stitching with normal tension easily creates raised pintucks. Cording also sta-bilizes, thereby reducing puckering. On sheer fabrics, the cord can be used to add color.

There are many methods for cording pintucks. Some machines have a hole in the needle plate (Bernina, Pfaff) or a guide that snaps onto the needle plate (Viking) through which the cording can be threaded. A dental-floss threader (see the sidebar at right) is often helpful for threading the cord, especially for thread-ing cord up through Bernina needle plates. (On Bernina 1630 machines, threading may be easier if you tip the machine back slightly.)

If you are comfortable bypassing bob-bin tension (this is especially easy to do on most Elnas), you can wind the cord onto the bobbin. Then thread the cord through the bobbin tension bypass hole, rather than into the usual tension slit; it will be caught in the pintuck as you stitch with the twin needles. Upper ten-sion may have to be tightened.

An easy and effective way to cord twin-needle stitching on any machine is to use a dental-floss threader.

1. First take a few stitches and stop with the needles down.
2. Raise the presser foot and lift the fabric.
3. Thread the cord under the fabric between the two needles (front to back)

Dental-floss threaders

Dental-floss threaders are designed for threading dental floss through orthodontics and bridge-work, but they work well as long, flexible plastic threaders for sewing. Use them to:

• thread cord up through the hole in Bernina's or Pfaff's needle plate, or through Viking's raised seam plate for corded twin-needle stitching (see the photo below);
• thread cord between the two needles to cord twin-needle pintucks on any machine;
• thread cord through the hole of a presser foot such as Bernina's embroi-dery foot, or Viking's, Elna's, and Pfaff's multiple-cord feet;
• thread cord or ribbon thread through the hole in the finger of Bernina's bobbin case;
• thread sergers.

You can purchase dental-floss threaders at drugstores. A package of 20 costs about $2. If you can't find them—they are usually displayed by the dental floss—check sev-eral drugstore chains or ask your dentist for a source.

Dental-floss threaders work well as long, flexible plastic threaders for sewing. One of their many practical uses is to thread cord up through the hole in Bernina's needle plate to cord twin-needle pintucks.

A simple method to cord twin-needle stitching on any machine is to take a few stitches and stop with the twin needles just into the fabric. Then raise the presser foot, lift the fabric, and use a dental-floss threader to thread cord between the needles.

there are a number of things you can do to compensate:

• spray-starching and pressing the fabric first;

• using new needles that are as close as possible to the ideal size (1.6/70), fine machine-embroidery cotton thread (such as Mettler 60/2 or DMC 50/2), and, if you have a choice, a seven- or nine-groove pintuck foot;

• shortening the stitch length;

• loosening (lowering) upper tension;

• sewing taut with a smooth, slow to medium speed.

Make sure the machine is clean. (Lint can cause tension problems). If there is still a problem, then you may have to compromise, either by loosening upper tension a little more and accepting a flatter tuck in order to prevent the puckering, or by cording the tuck with a fine cord, such as size 8 pearl cotton.

On polyester/cotton broadcloth, lengthwise rows of pintucks are especially difficult. Prewash, then lightly spray-starch and press the broadcloth. Follow the same guidelines as for Swiss batiste, except use new 2.0/80 twin needles with a five- or seven-groove pintuck foot and a medium-size cord, such as size 5 pearl cotton.

On some fabrics, including some broadcloth, it is virtually impossible to get acceptable, unpuckered lengthwise pintucks (be thankful you found out on your test sample!). The photo at left on the facing page) shows how different a lengthwise and crosswise pintuck can look. On a craft project, such as a pillow, you can change the grain direction when cutting the pattern so that the pintucks will be stitched crossgrain (assuming that on a test sample the crossgrain pintucks were fine). However, changing the direction a garment pattern piece is cut (for example, cutting a

using the dental-floss threader, as shown in the photo above.

4. Lower the presser foot.

5. Check that the cord is under the center groove of the foot. As you stitch, slightly lift the cord to keep it in this groove.

Pfaff has "cording tongues" in two sizes that snap onto the needle plate. They lift the fabric in front of the center groove of the pintuck foot (which Pfaff calls a "cording foot"). You can experiment with these cording tongues to put more fabric into the pintuck without using cord.

WORKING WITH DIFFICULT FABRICS

Some fabrics present special challenges for twin-needle stitching for which you may need to compensate and/or compromise. With challenging fabrics every factor is critical and must be as close to the ideal as possible.

For example, on very fine, soft fabrics, such as Swiss batiste, it is difficult to get crisp lengthwise uncorded pintucks without any puckering. However,

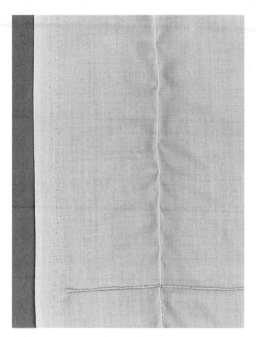

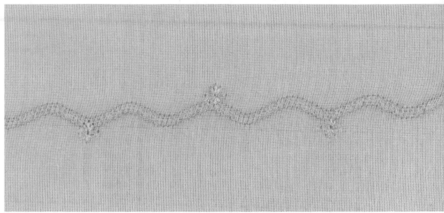

Uncorded lengthwise pintucks on lightweight fabric with no changes in thread, needles, and settings are likely to pucker, while crossgrain pintucks on the same fabric look fine.

blouse so that pintucks down the blouse front would be crossgrain) is not recommended because the fit and hang of the garment could be affected. So it may be necessary to change either your fabric choice or your design plan. Folded pintucks stitched with a straight stitch and a single needle might be successful even when twin-needle pintucks were not; but test to be sure.

Twin-needle shadow work

You can take advantage of the fact that the thread on the underside of twin-needle stitching zigzags between the two rows to create a shadow-work effect on sheer fabrics. This type of shadow work is effective around a skirt (or even for hemming the skirt); down the front of a blouse, pinafore, or an apron bib; on sleeves, collars, and so on. You can stitch a row on each side of pintucks or

fagoting to create a framing effect. Adding hand- or machine-stitched flowers, leaves, bows, and so forth can create the look of expensive imported embroideries (see the photo above).

Fabric: Sheer wovens that have body or that can be spray starched (or stiffened with another product) to give body. Swiss organdy is ideal.

Thread: Machine-embroidery cotton. The size should be appropriate for the fabric, usually 50/2 or 60/2. A darker color on the bobbin will create more shadow.

Needle: Twin needles 2.5mm apart have enough space between them for the shadow, yet are narrow enough to be used with a stitch with width. Experiment also with twin needles having other spacing, but remember that as the needles get farther apart, the stitch width must get narrower. Test carefully.

Foot: Basic zigzag or satin-stitch foot.

Stitch: Open, running type stitches with a shape such as tracery scallop (or arch), bracket, or serpentine (or multi-zigzag).

Experiment with other stitches. (Dense satin-type stitches can produce some interesting effects when stitched with twin needles, but they will not create a shadow work effect.)

On sheer fabrics, the bobbin thread of twin-needle stitching can create a shadow-work effect, as seen here with a serpentine stitch. Adding machine-stitched flowers gives the look of an expensive imported embroidery.

Tracery scallop

Bracket

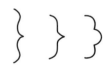

Serpentine Multi-zigzag

another spray-on or paint-on stiffening product. (A regular tearaway stabilizer should not used because it would be caught in the stitching and show through the sheer fabric.)

Some of the stitches for twin-needle shadow work can be corded with pearl cotton to create more shadow when using a longer stitch length. Thread the cord through the hole in the needle plate (Bernina, Pfaff) or wind pearl cotton on the bobbin and use the bobbin tension bypass hole (Elna) for the best results. On other machines, experiment. The shape of the stitch determines the ease of cording—more rounded stitches are easier to cord than stitches with sharp points.

A stitch width that is as wide as possible without hitting the presser foot usually gives the best look. Test the stitch width carefully. Here a tracery scallop stitch is used.

T I P

With all applications for twin needles, choose closely spaced, fine twin needles for lightweight fabrics and more widely spaced, larger twin needles for heavier fabrics. Loosen upper tension to keep fabric flat (a stabilizer may also be needed); tighten upper tension and/or cord the stitching for a raised effect. And always test the stitch width very carefully.

Width: As wide as possible without having one of the needles hit the foot or needle plate (see the photo above). Start with a width of about 2mm, then increase width carefully, testing all the way to the right and left through the stitch pattern, as explained on pp. 56-57.

Length: Varies with the stitch used, but must be relatively short for enough coverage on the underside.

Upper tension: Loosen (adjust to a lower number). (Loosening bobbin tension also creates "shadow" and can be done instead if you prefer.)

Stabilizer: Spray starch and press. For softer fabrics, do several applications of spray starching and pressing, or use

Other twin-needle work

On many fabrics that are unsuitable for pintucks, you can use twin needles and a straight stitch to add texture and dimension, especially if the stitching is corded. The resulting ridges can totally change the surface appearance, often giving a quilted look. It's fun to experiment with twin-needle stitching on different solid-color fabrics (even velveteen), as well as on prints. You can create a unique companion fabric to coordinate with the original fabric and use it for bodices, yokes, sleeves, collars, pockets, and accessories. The top photo on the facing page shows an example.

You can use twin needles and a straight stitch to stitch two perfectly even rows of topstitching or to attach both sides of a narrow ribbon or trim at the same time (see the middle photo on the facing page). These applications are suitable for most fabrics.

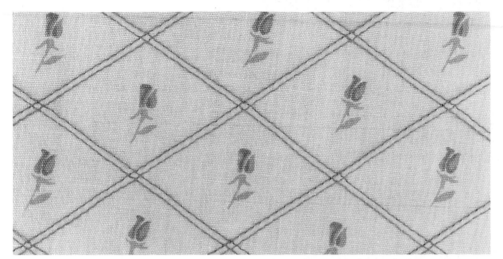

Twin-needle stitching can add texture and dimension to a fabric. In this example corded twin-needle stitching creates a diamond grid on a printed fabric.

You can also use twin needles with decorative stitches. The twin needles will create two rows of the stitch pattern that are either parallel to, adjoining, or overlapping each other, depending on the space between the needles and the stitch chosen.

Hemming is one of my favorite uses for twin needles (for a detailed discussion, see p. 122). For knits, the zigzag on the underside provides the needed stretch. Pintucks or decorative twin-needle stitching can be used to hem many fabrics. Either technique is a particularly useful treatment for sheer fabrics (like organdy), where a traditional hem would show through unattractively. They can also disguise the crease line of the previous hem when you let down a hem.

To hem with twin needles:
1. Press the hem allowance to the wrong side.
2. Stitch from the right side so that the stitching is at least ¼ in. from the raw edge of the hem allowance.
3. Trim the excess fabric up to the zigzag on the underside, as shown in the photo at right.

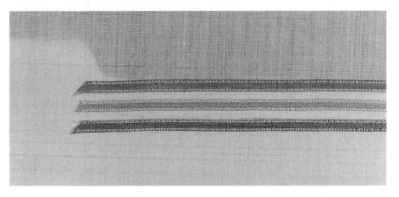

Twin needles and a straight stitch were used to attach both sides of narrow ribbon and at the same time re-hem the garment. (One of the three rows of ribbon covers the creaseline from the original hem.) Loosened upper tension and a basic zigzag foot kept the ribbon flat.

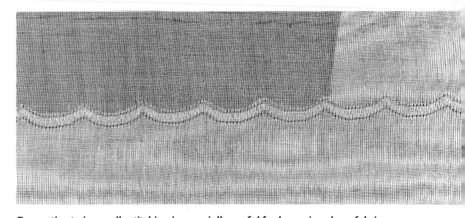

Decorative twin-needle stitching is especially useful for hemming sheer fabrics, such as organdy, where a traditional hem would show through. The hem is stitched from the right side, then excess fabric is trimmed up to the stitching on the underside.

Questions

How do you secure the beginning and end of twin-needle pintucks?

Ideally, twin-needle pintucks should be stitched on a piece of fabric larger than your pattern piece. After stitching the pintucks, block the fabric and staystitch just inside the cutting line to secure pintucks that run the full length or width of the pattern piece. Most of the time, the ends of the pintucks will be stitched again during construction, providing additional security.

Released pintucks are those that are not stitched the full length or width of the pattern piece; they are most often seen on the upper part of front bodices. Released pintucks do need to be secured. Leave long thread tails where the pintucks end. Pull the two top threads to the underside, using a pin to help. Knot the two top threads together along with the bobbin thread at the end of the tuck. (If you cannot tie all of these threads, tying any two of the three should be secure enough.) For extra neatness, thread all three threads into the eye of a hand needle, bury the thread tails in the underside of the pintuck for about ½ in., then cut off the excess thread.

I thought that for twin-needle work the two threads should be separated at the upper tension disc. Recently I heard instructions to put both threads on one side of the tension disc. Which is correct?

I recommend separating the two threads at the tension disc, then doing some test stitching with conditions the same as on the project. If the results are not satisfactory, and you are certain you are using the correct thread, a new needle of appropriate size, that your machine is clean, and so on, check that the upper threads are not twisted together. (On most machines, twisting would be obvious just above the needle bar.) If the threads are twisted, carefully rethread each thread separately: Take the thread from the right spool to the right side of tension disc and to the right needle, then the thread from the left spool to the left side of the tension disc and to the left needle. Also make sure the two threads do not rub together near the spools; either turn one spool over or use spool pins that keep the threads apart. If the stitching on the sides of the twin-needle stitch or pintuck still looks uneven, then experiment with different ways to thread (see the answer to the next question), including possibly putting both threads on the same side of the tension disc. All the sewing machine representatives I have consulted agree that in situations like this it's best to experiment and then do whatever works best.

My twin-needle stitching (especially on pintucks) looks fine on one side, but loose and uneven on the other side. How can I get the stitching on both sides to be acceptable?

First, follow the tips in the previous answer, including making sure that the twin needles are the correct system for your machine. But before trying both threads on the same side of the tension disc, try tightening upper tension to the point that it improves the loose side without causing puckering. It may also be helpful to increase tension on the thread that appears loose (by putting that thread through an additional guide at the top of the machine or on the needle bar), and/or reducing tension on the side that looks tight (take that thread out of either of these additional guides). If nothing seems to help, consult your dealer to see if the upper tension on your machine needs cleaning or adjustment.

Must twin-needle pintucks always be stitched in the same direction?

In keeping with the principles of directional stitching, this is usually best. (Directional stitching refers to the practice of stitching in a consistent direction to avoid distortion of the fabric.) For example, to stitch groups of pintucks on a blouse front, I usually stitch those in the center group first then work out to the sides using the grooves of a pintuck foot for perfect spacing, always stitching top to bottom.

There are exceptions, however. Occasionally I have seen pintucks that were closer together when stitched in one direction than in the other. In this case the grooves in the foot appeared equally spaced, so the needle bar may have been slightly off to one side. In cases like this, of course, you have to do what works best (at least until the machine is adjusted).

Stitching more than a few rows of pintucks distorts the shape of most fabrics, regardless of stitching direction. The pintucked fabric should be blocked before proceeding with cutting or other stitching.

The amount of fabric caught in my twin-needle pintucks is inconsistent. As I stitch I have to fight the tendency of more fabric being pulled into the tuck. Any suggestions?

If your presser foot has a wide opening in front, as some pintuck feet do, fabric can easily be drawn up into this open space, creating the problem you describe. Usually this can be remedied by switching to a presser foot that holds the fabric more securely in the front. If your machine company has a more closed pintuck foot, try it. For example, Viking has a seven-groove pintuck foot that is much more closed than their previous pintuck feet. If such a foot is not available for your machine, a foot

designed for another brand may work. (An adaptor and/or a different shank may be needed.) Another option is to substitute a traditional buttonhole foot and change the needle position to align with one of the two grooves. (Check that the needles will not hit the foot.)

How do you press twin-needle pintucks?

Twin-needle pintucks are not usually pressed to the side as are traditional folded (single-needle) pintucks. I do not press the twin-needle pintucks themselves, but rather the fabric next to them. (If the pintucks within a group are stitched very close together, then just press the fabric between each group of pintucks.) First spray starch and press the fabric up to the first pintuck. Lay the fabric over the edge of the ironing board so that the first tuck is just off the edge. Now you can press up to the next tuck. Continue in this way until done.

Your pintucks should not be puckered, but if they are, you may need to block them. Put straight pins through the ends of the tucks and into the ironing board to hold them straight and taut. Spray starch and let dry. Then, if necessary, press the fabric next to the tucks.

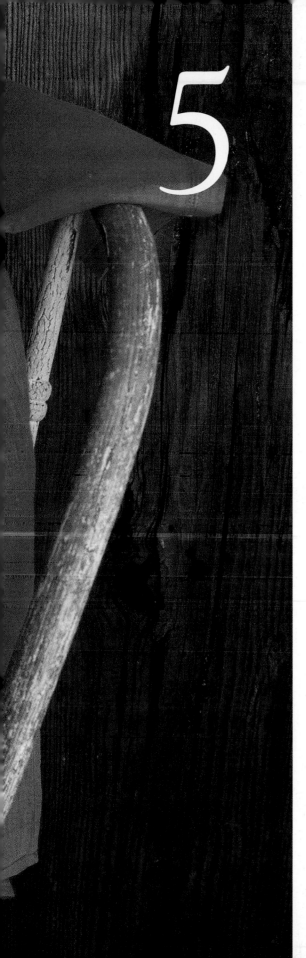

5 Hemstitching

Tone-on-tone detailing added to this purchased linen blouse accents its simple lines. Corded adjoining rows of hemstitching with a double wing needle embellish the front and the sleeves. Before hemstitching the front, several threads were withdrawn to make the needle holes more distinct. A decorative stitch completes the details.

The beautiful look of hemstitching, once attainable only by hand or with the use of one of the very scarce hemstitching machines, can now be created on most sewing machines. Hemstitching has a classic appeal that never goes out of style. You can see it on antique garments and linens, as well as on current designer blouses, dresses, nightgowns, and table and bed linens. Hemstitching is an excellent option if you want an heirloom look without the frills of delicate laces, ruffles, and puffing.

Hemstitching by hand entails withdrawing threads from the fabric and bundling the remaining parallel threads with a needle and thread to form an open design. It is often used as a decorative finish at a hem. Although it is possible to copy this look using the machine by first withdrawing threads by hand, then machine stitching the sides of the area (as was done on the blouse pocket shown on p. 75), in fact machine hemstitching has a much broader meaning. The term "hemstitching on the sewing machine" applies to sewing-machine versions of any of the following looks:

• the hand pin stitch (point de Paris), as used to attach lace (see the spoke collar in the photo at left on p. 92), to hem, and for Madeira appliqué;
• hemstitching as produced on hemstitching machines from the 1920s and 1930s;
• entredeux, a ladder-looking trim used in heirloom sewing to attach laces, fabrics, and embroideries (see the photo on p. 96);
• other stitching in which the open look or "holes" are the main decorative focus, as on the blouse collar shown in the photo on p. 80.

The following specifications apply to all hemstitching on the sewing machine:

Fabric: Wovens with a high percentage of linen or cotton and little or no polyester give the best results. Always stitch test samples. Sometimes unlikely fabric content or texture gives surprisingly excellent results. For example, some faille moiré (51% acetate, 49% cotton), chambray, and some cotton piqués hemstitch very well.

Fabrics with body, for example organdy, or those that can be spray-starched and pressed or stabilized to add body and crispness, give better results than very soft fabrics.

Thread: Fine machine-embroidery cotton gives excellent results. Rayon, silk, and other fine decorative threads can also be used. The thread must be very fine. Good choices in cotton are: Madeira 80/2, Zwicky 70/2, Mettler 60/2, and DMC 50/2.

Thread color should usually match fabric. A contrasting thread color is pleasing with some hemstitching techniques and stitches, such as the Parisian hemstitch, but unattractive with others. As always, testing is important.

Needle: Wing needles, double wing needles, or large Universal needles to help create the desired openings in the fabric (see the photo on the facing page). (Details on using the various needles are included with each hemstitching method.) Wing needles have metal extensions on each side that create very prominent holes. Use these with care—they can damage fine fabrics and laces.

Always test any wing or large Universal needles in your machine at a slow speed with a straight stitch first (see p. 55). Increase width carefully, if you want a wider stitch. If there is a clicking sound, the needle may be hitting something; do not use it until you check with your dealer.

Universal 120/19 needles have a larger than normal shank and can be difficult to get into the needle bar on some machines. Try several of these needles before giving up—they vary slightly, and sometimes out of a box of five, three will fit and two will not. If necessary, use the next smaller size (110).

Upper tension: Usually normal, but on heavier or stiffer fabrics, increase tension to create enough pull to open the holes, and on very lightweight or soft fabrics loosen tension slightly to prevent puckering.

Stabilizer: To avoid the puckering inherent in the use of such large needles, spray-starch and press the fabric several times until it is relatively stiff. Each time, spray a medium application of spray starch, then if possible, wait 15 to 30 seconds before pressing in order for the fibers to absorb the starch. (Saturating the fabric with spray starch can cause scorching.) Other spray-on or paint-on stiffeners can be used, but test them first.

With any of the following hemstitching conditions, a lightweight tear-away stabilizer may be needed under the fabric:
• stitching parallel to the lengthwise grain;
• hemstitching a long length;
• using more complicated hemstitches (those that have more steps in the pattern). For example, the Venetian hemstitch is more likely to need stabilizing than the Parisian;
• stitching multiple rows;
• stitching on corners, sharp curves, or multiple fabric layers, such as areas where cuffs, bands, or collars are attached;
• using a very soft or lightweight fabric that could not be adequately stiffened.

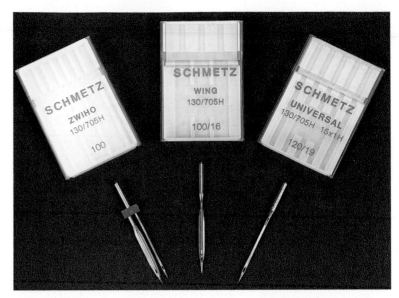

Needles used for hemstitching include, from left to right, the double wing needle, the wing needle, and the large Universal needle (size 120/19).

In addition to stabilizing, other ways to compensate for hemstitching's tendency to pucker include holding the fabric taut as you sew, loosening upper tension, shortening the stitch length, decreasing stitch width, using a metal presser foot rather than a lightweight plastic one, and using a smaller needle size (slightly less pronounced holes are better than puckered fabric).

Always test your stitching first on a fabric scrap, duplicating the conditions of the project.

Methods

There are three basic ways to achieve a hemstitched look on a sewing machine: double wing-needle adjoining rows, single wing-needle adjoining rows, and built-in hemstitches. When the fabric and application are appropriate, any of these three methods can be combined with withdrawing threads from the fabric to create a hand-hemstitched look.

DOUBLE WING-NEEDLE ADJOINING ROWS

A double wing needle can be used on most sewing machines with twin-needle capability to create a beautiful hemstitched effect (see the photo at left). Use it on fabrics appropriate for hemstitching either as a decorative topstitch (this can be through both the garment fabric and the facing) or to hem two layers (in this case the excess fabric is trimmed up to the zigzag stitching on the underside).

Needle: Double wing needle (also called twin wing or double hemstitch needle). This variation of a twin needle actually has one regular Universal needle and one wing needle, not two wing needles, as its name implies.

Foot: Use a foot that provides visibility, such as an open-toe satin-stitch foot, a foot with a transparent plastic front, or one with a large opening, such as Bernina's buttonhole foot #3.

Stitch: Straight. (Other stitches can be used also, but a simple straight stitch gives excellent results.)

Length: 2mm to 2.5mm

1. Holding the fabric taut, straight-stitch the desired distance.
2. With the needles and presser foot up, turn the fabric 180°.
3. Lower the needles into the fabric so that the wing needle falls precisely in the last hole it made. (The other needle will go into unstitched fabric.) Lower the presser foot.
4. Stitch the second row slowly and carefully, making sure the wing needle continues to hit the holes it made on the first row, as shown in the photo above right. Sew with one hand on the fabric behind the needle and one in front. Pull slightly to the back or front when slight adjustments are necessary.

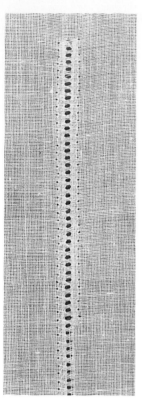

This hemstitching effect was created with a double wing needle and two passes of straight stitching. The lower part of the sample shows how the stitching appears after the first pass; the upper part shows the stitching completed.

For hemstitching using double wing needles, the second pass is stitched in the opposite direction of the first, with the wing needle hitting exactly in the holes it made on the first pass. Visibility is important. If you do not have an open-toe or transparent foot, use a foot with a large opening like this Bernina buttonhole foot.

As long as you hit the previous holes precisely most of the time, it is unlikely that occasional misses will be noticeable on the finished project. After the second pass is complete, there may be stray threads down the middle of the row of enlarged holes; these occur when the wing needle stitching on the second pass does not quite overlap the first row. These threads can be carefully picked out with a needle or pin and clipped at the ends.

Options

To give more definition and, on sheer fabrics, to add color, you can cord double wing-needle stitching just as for twin-needle stitching (see pp. 59-60). It's easiest to thread cord between double wing needles with a dental-floss

This hemstitching effect was created with a single wing needle and a simple zigzag stitch.

threader if you lower the needles just until the points pierce the fabric.

If it's practical, you can withdraw one or more threads from the fabric before pressing and stitching (see the photo on pp. 66-67 for an example). Doing so will make the holes even more distinct and easier to hit on the second pass, and it also reduces the likelihood of puckering. Stitch on each side of the drawn threads so that the wing needle goes into the area where the threads have been withdrawn and the regular needle goes into the undisturbed fabric.

SINGLE WING-NEEDLE ADJOINING ROWS

In order for the holes in machine hemstitching to stay open, there must be stitching holding or pulling the holes open from several directions: either from front and back, as well as the side, or from multiple diagonal directions. In double wing-needle hemstitching (explained above), the bobbin thread zigzagging on the back of the overlapping stitching pulls the holes open. With single wing needles, partially overlapping zigzag stitching can create the desired effect. The photo above shows a sample.

Because this method relies on a simple zigzag stitch, even the most basic zigzag machine can produce an elegant hemstitched effect. As with the double wing-needle method, two passes are required.

Needle: Size 100 wing needle or large Universal needle, usually size 120/19. For more delicate fabrics, Universal size 110/18 or smaller. (Size 120 wing needles should be used only on very loosely woven, sturdy fabrics, like those used for some table linens.)

Foot: Use a foot that provides visibility, such as an open-toe satin-stitch foot, a foot with a transparent plastic front, or one with a large opening, such as Bernina's buttonhole foot #3.

Stitch: Zigzag.
Width: 1.75mm to 2mm
Length: 1mm to 1.25mm

1. Stitch a row of zigzag stitching the length needed. Stop with the needle down on the left side.
2. Raise the presser foot. Turn the fabric 180° so that the line of stitching is now in front of the machine. Lower the presser foot.
3. Stitch a second row of zigzag stitching, guiding carefully so that each time the needle goes to the left, it hits

HEMSTITCHING WITH ZIGZAG STITCH

Stitched with a wing needle, a simple zigzag stitch becomes a decorative hemstitch.
(Arrows indicate stitching direction.)

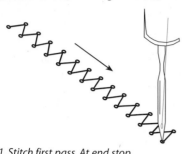

2. Turn fabric 180°.

3. Continue stitching. Left side of stitch enters holes on right side of previous stitching.

1. Stitch first pass. At end stop on left side with needle down.

Hemstitching can be done using a single wing needle and side-by-side passes of zigzag stitching. On the second pass, each stitch to the left hits a hole on the right side of the previous stitching.

exactly in the holes of what is now the right side of the previous row, as shown in the drawing above and the photo at left. Use a slow speed, and hold the fabric taut with one hand on the fabric behind the needle and one in front to adjust as necessary.

Options

When practical, before you press and stitch the fabric you can withdraw one or more threads from the area where the two rows will overlap. Doing so will make the holes more distinct.

You can also use other stitches. One that gives excellent results with this method is the picot (or "E") stitch, (width 2mm, length 2mm to 2.5mm). This stitch resembles the Parisian hemstitch, but since the holes are not pulled open by repeated steps in its pattern, pivoting and overlapping part of the stitch creates a more distinct and finished hemstitched effect. A sample is shown in the photo and drawing on the facing page.

BUILT-IN HEMSTITCHES

The third method for achieving the look of hemstitching using the sewing machine is with built-in hemstitches. Many machines have stitches that automatically stitch in and out of the same holes as required for hemstitching. With them the need for multiple passes over the line of stitches is eliminated. When I began teaching fine machine sewing techniques in 1982, only a few sewing machines had any really usable hemstitches. Today there are more than 30 machines available that have the two most popular and useful of the hemstitches—the Parisian stitch (resembling the pin stitch made by hand) and the Venetian stitch (resembling entredeux).

Needle: Most often, Universal size 120/19. Use smaller Universal needles (110/18, 100/16, 90/14, etc.) on more delicate fabrics, especially when replicating the hand version of pin stitching, where the holes should be only slightly enlarged. Size 100 wing needles may be used for more prominent holes on sturdy, loosely woven fabrics, like most linens. Wing needles can damage the fibers of fine fabrics and laces. Test first.

HEMSTITCHING WITH PICOT STITCH

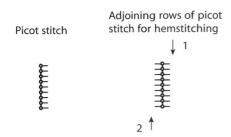

Arrows indicate direction of stitching.

The picot stitch can also be used for single wing-needle hemstitching. On the lower part, only the first pass has been completed; on the upper part, the second pass has been stitched as well.

Parisian

Venetian

Turkish

Four-sided

Rhodes

Picot

Daisy

Cross stitch

Foot: When possible use a foot that holds the fabric securely, such as the basic metal presser foot, to help reduce puckering. Stitches where thread builds up, like the Venetian stitch, may require a satin-stitch foot (preferably metal and not open toe) to allow the stitching to feed easily without getting crushed. On many Elnas, the multi-cord sole (used with or without cord) works well as a metal satin-stitch foot.

Stitch: Consult your sewing-machine manual for any information on stitches for hemstitching. Usually the hem-stitches are grouped together. Even if there are no stitches specified in the manual, look for and try stitches that have forward and reverse as well as sideways stitching in their pattern and that repeatedly stitch in and out of the same holes. The most common built-in hemstitches are:

• Parisian (also called pin stitch, point de Paris)—The stitch pattern resembles the letter "L" (or a reversed "L"), repeating the vertical stitches and, on some machines, also the horizontal stitch.

• Venetian—The stitch pattern goes repeatedly around a diamond shape, as well as vertically from the top to the bottom of the diamond; it can resemble entredeux, especially when corded.

• Turkish—The Turkish stitch resembles the double overlock except each step in the pattern is repeated.

• Four-sided—The stitch pattern goes repeatedly around a square or rectangular shape.

• Rhodes—The Rhodes stitch resembles the honeycomb stitch, except each step in the pattern is repeated.

Other stitches that can produce a hemstitched look are:

• Picot—Similar to the Parisian stitch, but no part of the stitch is repeated.

• Daisy.

• Cross stitch—A cross stitch can resemble the Venetian stitch if the needle goes into rather than across the center intersection.

Width and length: Vary with stitch. (Settings for some machines are listed in Appendix C.) The most common settings for the two most used stitches are:

• Parisian—width 2mm, length 2mm to 2.5mm;

• Venetian—width 3mm to 4mm, length 2.5mm (except 1.3mm with the long-stitch button on Bernina 1130 and 1230).

Balancing alignment

For beautiful hemstitching, it is critical that the needle hit precisely in the same hole or holes as it repeats parts of the stitch pattern. Thankfully, the stitches often align perfectly and no adjustment is needed. But if they are misaligned at all, the holes will not be distinct or there will be stray threads across them, as you can see in the photo at right. Since stitch alignment can be affected by the type of fabric, number of fabric layers, grain direction, stabilizer, and so on, many machines have a balancing feature to adjust the stitch.

Consult the machine manual for instructions on balancing, adjusting, or fine-tuning stitches. Stitch at a slow speed and watch the forward and reverse parts of the stitch. If the needle comes forward too far and overshoots a hole it should hit, shorten the forward stitches by adjusting toward minus (-). If the needle goes back too far for the hole it should hit, adjust toward plus (+). (On Pfaffs, the stitches are adjusted the reverse: If the needle comes too far forward, adjust toward plus [+] to compress the stitch; if the needle goes too far back, adjust toward minus [-] to spread the stitch.)

When you get the stitch aligned perfectly, make notes on your sample. Sketch the adjusted position of the fine-tuner or note the number of times you pressed (+) or (-). Save your samples and notes in your notebook. The next time you have a similar fabric combination, the adjustment will likely be the same or very close.

It will take some practice to be comfortable with balancing stitches, but it is worth the effort to learn to fine-tune stitching. It will allow you to perfect hemstitching, as well as other stitching where alignment is critical, such as the double overlock stitch, decorative stitches like the daisy or star, letters and numbers, and on many machines, buttonholes.

If your machine does not have a fine-tuning feature and the stitches are not perfectly aligned, try additional stabilizing, either by applying more spray starching and pressing or by using a tearaway stabilizer underneath. Also experiment with stitch length and with mirror imaging, since these may also slightly affect the alignment.

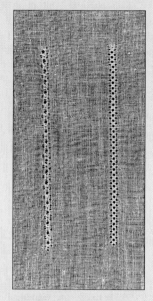

If a stitch is not balanced properly, the holes will not be distinct (stitching at left). After balancing (stitching at right), the look is clean and open.

Note that on most machines the automatic settings for hemstitches are generally too wide and long and should be narrowed and shortened.

Stitching a test sample with conditions exactly the same as the project, including the same fabric, number of layers, stabilizer, thread, needle, stitch length and width, presser foot, and even grain direction, is most important for hemstitching. If the enlarged holes are not clean and distinct or if threads cross them, the stitch alignment probably needs balancing (see the sidebar above).

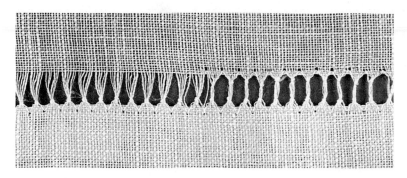

In this sample of a hem treatment, threads were withdrawn from an area about ¼ in. wide, then the Parisian stitch was worked along the hem side, bundling the stitches and securing the hem (left). Parisian stitching has been worked along part of the top edge of the withdrawn threads, creating parallel bars across the open area (right).

Options   If you wish to combine machine and hand hemstitching, you can withdraw threads from the fabric either before or after stitching two parallel rows about ¼ in. to ½ in. apart.

When threads are withdrawn before stitching, you can stitch hemstitches or other machine stitches (especially overlock stitches) along each side of the open area, as was done on the blouse in the photo at right. You can use a smaller needle for this than when hemstitching without withdrawing threads. The parallel threads remaining in the open area can be grouped attractively either by the machine stitching on the sides or by hand. Parisian hemstitching is very effective for grouping the threads if you have the forward and reverse stitches of the pattern going just into the open area and the stitch to the side going into the fabric. Experiment with the second row of stitching: If the stitches on the second side are directly opposite those on the first, you will create parallel bars of threads in the open area (as in the photo above); if the stitches on the second side are offset, you will create zigzag bars of thread.

The other way to combine hand and machine hemstitching is to hemstitch two rows on grain and then withdraw the parallel threads between them afterward. Space the rows as desired. You can then group the remaining threads by hand with a needle and thread.

The Parisian hemstitch adds wonderful detail to this purchased linen blouse. Threads were withdrawn from the pocket, and the remaining threads were outlined with the hemstitch: the forward and reverse stitches on the threads, the side stitches catching the fabric edge. An additional row of the hemstitching adds a topstitched look to the pocket hem. The simple edging on the collar and cuffs is sewn so the stitch to the side just clears the edge of the fabric.

Test and balance the stitch without cord first, then add the cord and make additional adjustments, if necessary.

Sudden changes in speed can affect the alignment of built-in hemstitches. Stitch with a smooth, even sewing rhythm at a medium speed.

A dental-floss threader is helpful for threading cord through holes in a foot. Fabric under the foot keeps the threader from going down into needle-plate openings.

Withdrawing threads gives an exquisite effect, but it requires on-grain hemstitching—no curves or angles—and some time. An option that has many more application possibilities is a technique adapted from the hand appliqué cord technique.

Corded hemstitching

The description of appliqué cord in Margaret Pierce's *Heirloom Sewing II* (available from Margaret Pierce, Inc., P.O. Box 4542, Greensboro, NC 27404; 910-292-6430) inspired me to adapt this hand sewing technique to the sewing machine. For appliqué cord by hand, the pin stitch is used to couch cord on two facing adjoining rows. It creates the look of delicate entredeux inserted into the fabric. The machine technique is similar to an option shown for hemstitching with the single wing needle, where adjoining rows are stitched with the picot stitch (see pp. 72-73). To replicate appliqué cord, the side stitches on both passes couch cord. The machine version

can look remarkably like appliqué cord by hand.

Experimenting with cording these and other hemstitches, both single and adjoining rows, and with different sizes and colors of cord, opened a world of creative options for the hemstitching capabilities of sewing machines. Hemstitching over cord is much more visible and looks more finished, and it permits the use of more color than hemstitching without cord. Cording also adds strength and stability. The look can be delicate or bold (see the bottom photos on p. 78), depending on the cords used.

Cord: Multiple strands of thread or floss for a delicate look; for more visibility, size 5, 8, or 12 pearl cotton (the higher the number, the finer the cord), buttonhole twist/topstitching thread, or any similar cord that is colorfast and shrink resistant. Some of the wider hemstitches, like the Turkish and four-sided stitches, can also be stitched over very narrow (1/16-in. to 1/8-in. wide) ribbon. Cord color should usually match thread color. (If an exact match is not possible, choose thread a shade lighter than the cord. This is an exception to the usual rule for thread selection, but it works better in this case.) With hemstitches other than the Venetian, a cord color that contrasts with the thread may also be pleasing. Experiment.

Foot: Feet with holes or grooves to guide the cord(s) are very helpful. (A dental-floss threader makes it easier to thread cord through holes in a presser foot, as shown in the photo at left.) A foot to guide only one cord is needed with the Parisian, picot, four-sided, and Turkish hemstitches. For the Venetian hemstitch, which stitches over two slightly separated cords at the same time, use a foot that guides cords just left and right of center.

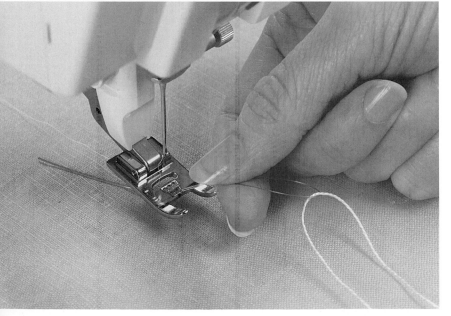

Try the cording or multiple-cord foot, buttonhole foot with two grooves, pin-tuck foot, and braiding foot. Experiment with others. A single cord can be fed through the curl of a narrow hemmer (use a hemmer not designed for straight stitching only). Feel the underside of presser feet. The underside of Pfaff's "fancy-stitch" foot #1A has two grooves that work well for guiding cord. If necessary, use a satin-stitch foot and guide the cords manually. When stitching adjoining rows, a foot that also provides some visibility in front is ideal.

Keep in mind that if the needle position on your machine can be changed when doing hemstitches, you can move the stitch to align with holes or grooves on feet, if necessary.

Stabilizer: Same as for hemstitching without cord, except that at the beginning and end of the corded hemstitching, a lightweight tearaway stabilizer under the fabric may also be needed.

PARISIAN OR PICOT STITCH OVER CORD

Both the Parisian hemstitch (also called the pin stitch or point de Paris) and the picot stitch are attractive when stitched over cord (see the photos above right). Their forward and reverse stitches should be right next to the cord, and the stitches to the side should go just over the cord. With the Parisian stitch the holes will be more prominent because of the repeated stitches.

If your machine does not have the Venetian hemstitch (which allows you to stitch over both cords at the same time), you can replicate the hand appliqué cord technique with the Parisian hemstitch or the picot stitch on two adjoining rows.
1. Stitch a row of the Parisian hemstitch or picot stitch so that the stitch to the side goes over the cord to couch it.

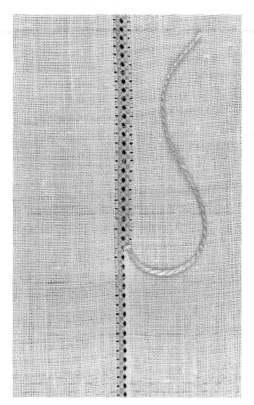

The Parisian or the picot stitch is effective when stitched over cord, whether as a single row (bottom of photo) or as two adjoining rows (top of photo).

Experiment with different feet and note which one is most helpful for guiding the cord; for this application, the foot ideally allows some visibility for hitting the same holes on the reverse pass.
2. At the end of the row, pivot and stitch a second row, partially overlapping the first, as shown in the photo above right. (Pivot, with the needle down, immediately before or after the stitch to the side. For machines that take two stitches to the side, pivot after the first one.) The cord goes around the needle when you pivot. The forward and reverse stitches on the second side must hit exactly the same holes as the forward and reverse stitches made on the first pass. The stitch to the side goes over the cord, as before.

Two adjoining rows of the Parisian or picot stitch over cord replicate the hand appliqué cord technique. The forward and reverse stitches on the second pass hit the holes created on the first pass. The stitch to the outside couches cord on both passes.

With the Venetian hemstitch you can stitch over two cords at the same time. A multiple-cord foot makes it easy to guide the cords just left and right of center.

CORDED VENETIAN HEMSTITCH

If your machine has the Venetian hemstitch, you do not need to pivot and stitch a second row. You can stitch one row of the Venetian hemstitch over two cords simultaneously, as shown in the photo above, and create the same look as that of adjoining rows of the Parisian hemstitch. Each side of the Venetian hemstitch couches a cord; the enlarged holes are down the center between the two cords. Look for a foot to guide the cords just left and right of center, such as the multiple-cord foot or a buttonhole foot with two grooves.

The photos at right show examples of corded hemstitching. With size 8 pearl cotton or buttonhole twist/topstitching thread, the corded Venetian hemstitch resembles entredeux. The corded Venetian hemstitch is also very effective for fagoting (see pp. 110-113).

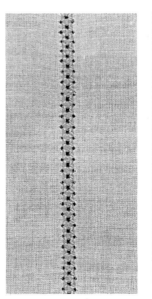
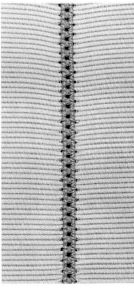

The Venetian hemstitch on Swiss batiste with a 110 needle corded with four strands of thread has a delicate look (left). On cotton piqué with size 5 pearl cotton and a wing needle, it has a bolder look (right).

FOUR-SIDED OR TURKISH HEMSTITCHES OVER CORD OR RIBBON

Four-sided and Turkish hemstitches create an interesting decorative effect when stitched over cord or ribbon (see the two stitch-sample photos at right). Over ribbon, they can create the look of beading. Adjust the stitch width so it just clears the cord or ribbon.

STARTING AND ENDING CORDED HEMSTITCHING

The beginning and the end of corded hemstitching are often hidden in a seam. In situations where they will show, leave long tails of cord at each end. Thread each cord tail into the large eye of a hand needle with a needle threader. Take it to the back of the fabric and weave it into the stitches for about ⅜ in., as shown in the photo at right. Then trim the excess cord.

An option with the Venetian hemstitch is to start stitching with a loop of cord pulled taut around the needle.

Hemstitching at corners

Many hemstitching applications necessitate turning corners. For example, when hemming or attaching lace around a square collar or using hemstitching to appliqué any shapes with points you need to be able to turn corners neatly.

The double wing-needle hemstitching method is effective and attractive for hemming (see the photo on p. 80). To turn the corner of the outer row of stitching when using this method (as would be required on a square collar), "walk" the outside needle (the Universal needle) around the corner for one or two stitches, with the wing needle hitting the same corner hole each time. (To "walk," lift the presser foot enough

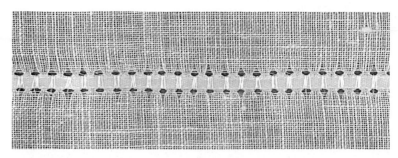

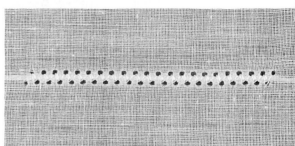

Stitched over ribbon, the four-sided stitch creates the look of beading, as shown above. The Turkish hemstitch may also be stitched over ribbon, or over pearl cotton, as shown at right.

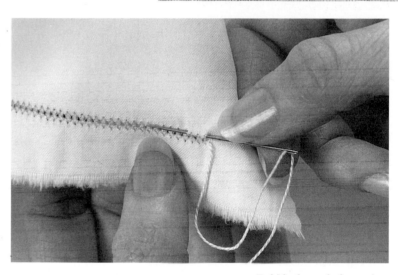

To hide the end of a cord, weave it in the stitches on the wrong side of the fabric for about ⅜ in.

to move the fabric, lower it, then manually turn the flywheel toward you for each stitch.) On the inner row of stitching, the wing needle must again hit the same corner hole while you walk the Universal needle to turn the corner, so the inner stitches must overlap for a stitch or two. With such fine thread, these stitches will not be noticeable.

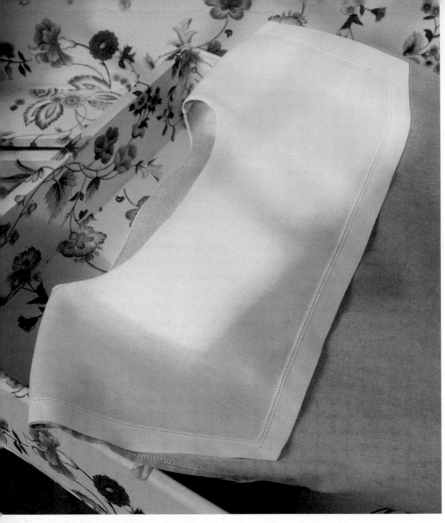

The crisp white collar of a middy blouse is hemstitched with adjoining rows of straight stitching using a double wing needle. Excess fabric is trimmed up to the stitching on the underside of the single-fold hem.

TURNING A CORNER WITH THE VENETIAN HEMSTITCH

The Venetian hemstitch can be cornered in one or two steps.

ONE-STEP METHOD

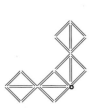

Stop at end of stitch pattern. Turn fabric 90°; continue stitching.

TWO-STEP METHOD

1. Stop before corner.

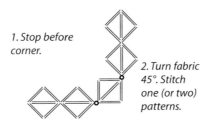

2. Turn fabric 45°. Stitch one (or two) patterns.

3. Stop and turn fabric 45°. Continue stitching.

In general, with any of the built-in hemstitches, turn the corner at the end of the stitch pattern(as was done on the collar of the blouse in the photo on the facing page). Since these stitches are formed differently on different machines, it is best to practice cornering with the hemstitches on your machine and make careful notes.

Machines that have the option of stopping automatically at the end of the stitch pattern usually stop at the correct point for pivoting and turning. Simply engage this feature along with the needle-down option during the last stitch before the turn. When the machine stops, raise the presser foot, turn the fabric, lower the foot and continue. If the machine does not stop at the right place to turn the corner, I usually use this feature anyway, then tap the foot pedal as many times as necessary to get to the best pivot point. For example, the Elna 7000, 9000, and Diva stop at the left point of the diamond pattern on the Venetian hemstitch. Tap the foot pedal twice to get to the low point of the diamond, then pivot to turn.

Unless a sharp corner is absolutely needed, with the Venetian hemstitch I like to turn the corner in two steps, stitching a short diagonal across the point as shown in the drawing at left. Stop at the end of the stitch pattern just before the corner, turn the corner halfway (45°), stitch one or two complete stitch patterns, then turn another 45° to complete the corner.

Use a lightweight tearaway stabilizer under the fabric whenever turning corners with cord. When turning a corner with corded Venetian hemstitching where both sides of the stitch are being corded at the same time, the outside cord covers more distance than the inside cord; to compensate, give a slight tug on the inside cord to take up the slack. With most of the other hemstitches, keep the cord to the outside of the needle when pivoting.

With sharp curves you may have to stop repeatedly and pivot at the end of the stitch pattern. This may not be necessary with more gradual curves. Test by stitching a similar curve on a scrap before stitching the project.

Applications

Hemstitching is one of my favorite embellishments because of its classic look and because of the unbelievable number of decorative as well as practical ways it can be used. With all the different hemstitching methods and variations, including cording, the range of creative possibilities is almost endless.

Suitable patterns are easy to find. The main criterion is that they be designed for fabrics appropriate for hemstitching.

The time I can devote to sewing is limited, as it is for so many sewers, so I look for ready-to-wear garments of acceptable fabric, quality, and price to individualize with hemstitching and other embellishments. More than once I have seen hemstitched designer blouses for $150 or so and the same, or very similar, blouse without hemstitching on sale for $35 or $40. Of course, I buy the basic blouse and hemstitch it myself. You can hemstitch the collar, pocket(s), cuffs, placket, hem (including short-sleeve hems), folded tucks, or around the neck and armbands, or any appropriate combination of these. On purchased garments, first test the stitching on an area that will not show, such as a seam allowance or the lower part of a blouse that will be tucked in. You can also hemstitch purchased linens to give them a designer heirloom look.

The Venetian hemstitch sewn over blue cord highlights the collar and the edges of a bow on a classic white piqué blouse. The same detailing is repeated on the hem of the sleeves.

In general, almost any hemstitch can be used to decorate a single or double layer of fabric, such as for topstitching or for a single-fold hem. The Parisian hemstitch is usually the best choice to hemstitch a folded or finished edge, such as a double-fold hem or to appliqué ribbon.

Almost any application stitched from the right side of the fabric may also be corded to add visibility, color, strength, stability, or a more finished appearance. (With the four-sided or Turkish hem-

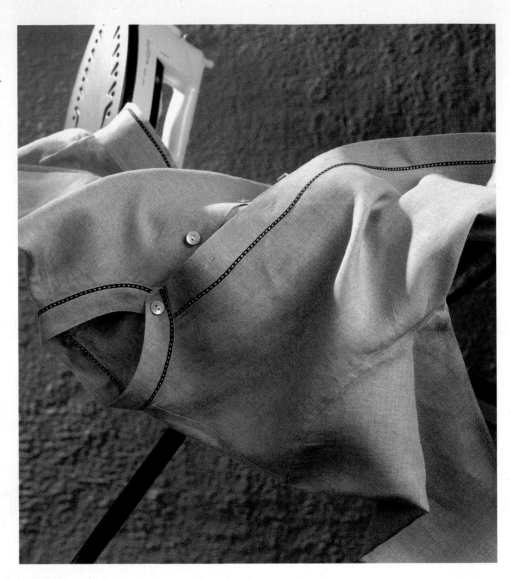

TIP

Never hemstitch right on a raw edge because the stitching would not be secure. Instead either hemstitch at least ¼ in. from the raw edge and trim up to it, or hemstitch over a folded edge.

stitches, an alternative is to stitch them over a narrow ribbon or trim.) An additional option is to weave cord, floss, or very narrow ribbon through the stitches or the holes after stitching (see the photo above).

TOPSTITCHING AND OTHER ROWS OF DECORATIVE STITCHING

You can embellish collars, yokes, bodices, blouse fronts, pockets, cuffs, sleeves, the lower edges of skirts, and so on with one or more separate rows of hemstitching. For example, the Turkish hemstitch was used as a decorative topstitch on the collar, cuffs and pocket flaps of the purchased red blouse shown in the photo on p. 84.

FACINGS AND PLACKETS

One practical as well as decorative use for hemstitching is to embellish a garment and finish its facings at the same time, for example, around a jewel neck opening or on a placket. To hemstitch a garment and its unfinished facing, stitch from the right side through both layers, staying at least ¼ in. to ½ in. from the

A purchased linen dress gets an easy and elegant detail: a Parisian hemstitch sewn down both sides of the front facings. The lower edge of the dress (not visible in the photo) is narrow hemmed and Parisian hemstitched in one step.

raw edge of the facing underneath. Then trim the excess facing fabric up to the stitching on the underside.

A facing whose outer edge has been folded under can be hemstitched with the Parisian hemstitch or picot stitch, as was done on the front facings of the dress shown in the photo on p. 83. Position the fabric so that the forward and reverse stitches are on the single layer of fabric next to the facing and the stitch to the side catches the facing. (This can usually be stitched from the wrong side so that the facing is visible during stitching.) An interesting variation is to make the facings a design element, putting them on the outside of the garment, like neck and arm bands. They can match or contrast with the garment color (see the top photo on p. 95).

ADJOINING ROWS

Multiple adjoining rows of hemstitching can create some wonderful effects (see the bottom photos on the facing page). If you plan to stitch an area wider than two or three adjoining rows, do the hemstitching on a separate piece of fabric. Then cut the hemstitched fabric to shape and appliqué it onto the project. The fabric under the appliqué may be trimmed away.

Parisian and picot adjoining rows
With the Parisian and picot hemstitches, you can stitch the adjoining rows so that the stitches to the side go to the outside on the adjoining rows and the forward and reverse stitches overlap (as in the single wing-needle adjoining rows). You can also stitch them in the opposite direction, so that the stitches to the side meet in the center between the rows. Both methods, shown in the drawing below, create attractive effects.

The Turkish hemstitch adds a tailored finish to the outer edge of the collar of a classic linen blouse. The same detailing, repeated on upper edges of the pocket flap and cuffs, gives an easy and elegant finish to this purchased garment.

PARISIAN AND PICOT ADJOINING ROWS

Either side of the Parisian and picot stitches can adjoin.

The forward and reverse stitches can overlap (left) or the stitches to the side can overlap (right).

First row   ↓   ↓   First row

↑   Second row   Second row   ↑

Arrows indicate direction of stitching.

Venetian adjoining rows

Two adjoining rows of corded Venetian hemstitching can resemble double entredeux. (Double entredeux looks like two side-by-side rows of entredeux.) I used this technique on the collar and sleeves of the blue linen blouse shown on the cover of this book to make the hemstitching more visible.

Stitch the first row as usual over two cords so that the large holes are between the cords (see p. 78).

Stitch the second row so that it overlaps one side of the first row. The stitches to one side of the second row go over one cord and into the large holes of the first row of stitching. Therefore, you need to cord only the outside edge of the second row, as shown in the photo at right. You can stitch additional rows the same way.

Turkish, Rhodes, and four-sided adjoining rows

Multiple adjoining rows of the Turkish, Rhodes or four-sided stitches create an effective machine version of a hand pulled-thread effect called fil tiré. Usually the multiple rows are stitched on a separate piece of well-starched or stabilized fabric, then cut out and appliquéd onto background fabric.

Some of these stitch patterns end on the left and are easier to work if you start on the right side of the fabric and add rows to the left. Others end on the right and are best stitched left to right. For example, for a stitch pattern that ends on the right:

1. Start on the left side of the fabric. At the end of the first row, stop with the needle down at the end of the stitch pattern on the right. Use the automatic

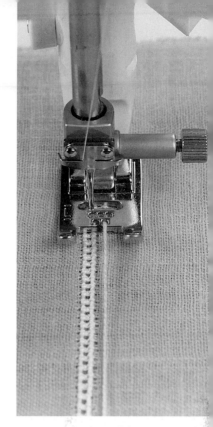

Two adjoining rows of the corded Venetian hemstitch can resemble double entredeux. The first row is stitched over two cords as usual. For the second row, only one additional cord is needed.

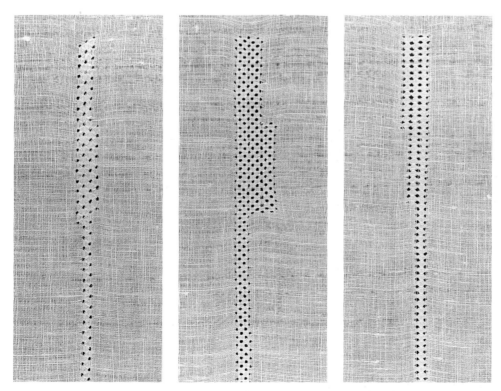

Adjoining rows of the Turkish (left), Rhodes (middle) or four-sided hemstitches (right) can be used to create a pulled-thread effect called fil tiré.

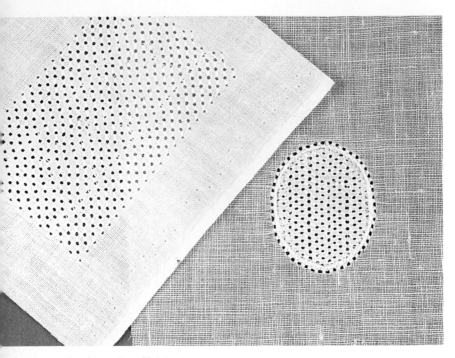

For this project, fil tiré (adjoining rows of Rhodes, Turkish, or four-sided hemstitches) was first worked over an oversized area (left sample). Then the oval shape was cut out and appliquéd to the background fabric with both a corded satin stitch and the Parisian hemstitch.

a similar work is shown in the photo at left. Proceed as follows:

1. Trace the desired design shape onto a small, very well-starched piece of linen. It is best to keep the design small (no larger than about 2 in. by 1½ in.) and simple, like an oval or a diamond shape.
2. Stitch multiple adjoining rows of the Rhodes hemstitch (with a 120 Universal needle) to cover the traced design and extend about ¼ in. beyond the shape. You can substitute the Turkish or four-sided stitch.
3. Remove the markings. Spray-starch and press the fabric to block it. Trace the design onto the stitched area again.
4. Staystitch on the traced line using a short straight stitch and a regular needle (80 Universal), then cut out the design.

end-of-pattern option, if your machine has it. Otherwise, stop manually.
2. Pivot the fabric 180°. Stitch the second row so that the rightmost stitches hit exactly into the leftmost stitches of the previous row. The open-toe foot and a slow speed are very helpful for this. Disengage the needle-down option for this step so you can adjust guiding as needed.
3. Stop manually at the end of this row on the left. Pivot the fabric, and continue in this way for as many rows as needed to cover the desired space.

One of my favorite fil tiré projects was one I designed for a class. It combines fil tiré with both satin stitch and Parisian hemstitch appliqué techniques;

Now appliqué the fil tiré design onto a larger piece of linen, as follows:
1. Stitch the design in place using a corded satin stitch with a lightweight tearaway stabilizer underneath (stitch width about 2mm, length about .6mm, size 5 pearl cotton for the cord, fine cotton thread, and size 80 needle). The cord should be just onto the edge of the fil tiré design.
2. If you wish, trim the fabric (and the tearaway stabilizer) from behind just the appliqué. A loosely woven fabric will be more secure if left untrimmed.
3. Stitch another pass, this time with the Parisian hemstitch (stitch width about 2mm, length about 2.5mm, 120 needle, open-toe or satin-stitch foot). The forward and reverse stitches are just outside the satin stitch, and the stitch to the side goes over the cord and onto the fil tiré.

FOLDED TUCKS

Folded tucks, from narrow ones to wide pleat-like ones, can be attractively hemstitched with the Parisian hemstitch or the picot stitch, as was done on the blouse in the photo on p. 97.

1. Fold and stitch the tuck as usual. Use fine thread, a regular needle, and a normal straight stitch.

2. Press the tuck in the desired direction.

3. Parisian hemstitch (most often with a 120 needle) over the stitched line. The forward and reverse stitches are on the single layer of fabric next to the tuck and the stitch to the side goes just onto the tuck itself, as shown in the photo at right. The original straight stitching should not show enough to have to be removed.

APPLIQUÉING FOLDED OR FINISHED EDGES

The Parisian hemstitch (or the picot stitch) can be used to appliqué folded or finished edges to resemble hand pin stitching, as shown in the photo below.

Use it to appliqué ribbon, trims, and embroideries, including shaped embroidered medallions. If the trim or medallion is sheer, you can trim away the fabric under it for a more open effect. (A loosely woven fabric will be more secure if left untrimmed.) Use the Parisian hemstitch on the folded edges of delicate appliqué pieces to resemble Madeira appliqué. Hemstitch from the right side so that the stitch to the side catches the appliqué and the forward and reverse stitches creating the large holes are alongside the appliqué.

SHADOW APPLIQUÉ

The elegance of hemstitching can easily be combined with the beauty of shadow appliqué. Because of its sheerness and body, imported organdy is ideal for this technique. You can also use other sheer fabrics, such as Swiss batiste, if they are sufficiently spray-starched and pressed or put in a hoop; also use a smaller needle. Both layers of fabric can be the same color, or you can use a darker fabric under a lighter one. I usually use the

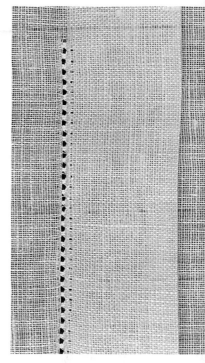

Folded tucks are attractive with Parisian hemstitching. The hemstitching is done after the tuck has been stitched and pressed.

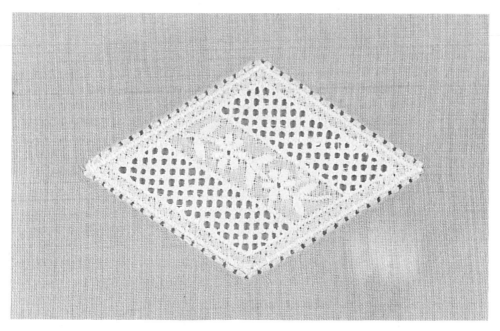

When the Parisian hemstitch is used for appliquéing, the effect is of hand pin stitching. The fabric under sheer appliqués may be trimmed away for a more open effect.

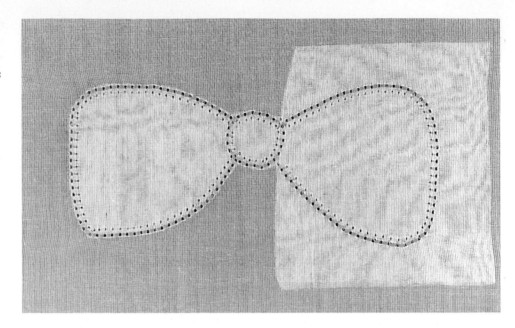

For this shadow appliqué, blue organdy was placed under white organdy, then the Parisian hemstitch was stitched from the top following a traced design. The excess fabric is then trimmed from the back (as has been done at left).

TIP

When mixing different fabrics on a project, always prewash them (see p. 7). Otherwise you risk unsightly puckering if one fabric shrinks more than another on the finished project.

same fabric for both layers, but a non-sheer fabric could be used for the underlayer.

1. Trace the design onto the top piece of fabric.

2. Lay this over the other fabric and pin in place.

3. Hemstitch from the top side following the design as shown in the photo above. You can use almost any hemstitch, but if the shape of the design is small, a narrow hemstitch like the Parisian or Venetian gives better results than a wide stitch.

4. Carefully trim away the fabric around the design from the back. (For a variation, you can trim the fabric from inside the design instead, leaving the double layer of fabric surrounding the design.)

ATTACHING LACE TO FABRIC

When you use sewing-machine hemstitching to attach lace to fabric, the stitching can resemble hand pin stitching, entredeux, hemstitching from old hemstitching machines, or just a pretty embroidered open effect (see the collars and pinafore-style bib shown in the photo at left on p. 92). Hemstitching the lace can be a real problem-solver, especially when you are attaching lace in shapes, such as loops, teardrops, and so on—applications where attaching lace with entredeux and traditional machine heirloom techniques is difficult.

In most cases either of two very practical and easy methods can be used to attach lace to fabric with hemstitching. With the first method, the lace is positioned in place, the lace headings are hemstitched to the fabric, and the fabric behind the lace is trimmed. This method is ideal for attaching shaped lace (with curved edges, loops, and so on). Most of the hemstitching techniques and stitches can be used with this method, but the Parisian and Venetian stitches are especially appropriate since they resemble hand pin stitching and entredeux respectively. Cording the stitches is also an option.

The second method involves hemstitching, usually with the Parisian (or picot) stitch, over a folded fabric edge next to the lace. This method is much

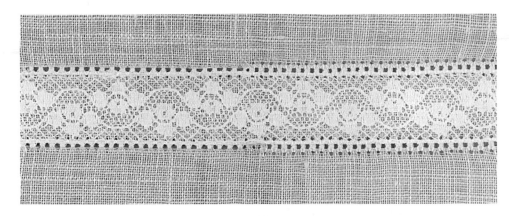

Hemstitching is a practical and attractive way to attach lace to fabric. With the first method the lace is positioned, then the headings are hemstitched to the fabric. Two suitable stitches are the Parisian stitch (left) and the Venetian stitch (right).

more secure, a factor that is a consideration when you are attaching lace to stress areas on a garment or if hard wearing and washing are likely.

There is a third method. Briefly, this method involves hemstitching about ½ in. from the fabric edge, trimming the fabric, then zigzagging the lace to the hemstitching right sides up. One side of the zigzag stitch goes into a hole of the hemstitching; the other side goes just across the lace heading. I rarely use this method because it involves extra steps and because the thread from the zigzag stitching often shows. Only the first two methods will be covered in more detail with reference to the applications that follow.

Needle: Most often, Universal size 120/19. Use smaller Universal needles (110/18, 100/16, 90/14, etc.) on more delicate fabrics, especially for the look of hand pin stitching. Wing needles can damage laces; test carefully.

Lace: For best results, use laces with a high percentage of cotton. For a less frilly look, choose more tailored or heavier laces, such as Cluny lace or tatting. Any lace that will not be gathered should be spray-starched and pressed carefully without stretching. If it will be applied straight, press it as straight as possible. If it will be attached to a curve,

shape it into a similar curve, press, let cool, and handle with care to maintain the shape. (Spray starching and pressing also preshrink the lace, which is especially important with tatting and Cluny laces.)

Insertion laces Insertion laces are straight on both edges and are "inserted" within the garment rather than along an edge. They are applied straight or in shapes almost anywhere on a garment—yokes, sleeves, skirts, and so on.

With either the first or second method, first stitch the lace onto the fabric in the desired position with a straight stitch (length 2mm) along both headings. Use a regular needle (size 60 or 70), a basic zigzag presser foot, and the same fine thread you will use for hemstitching. Then switch to the desired hemstitch needle.

To use the first method of attaching lace to fabric, hemstitch along each edge of the lace so that one side of the stitch goes just over the lace heading and the rest of the stitch is on the fabric. The large holes of the stitch should be on the fabric right next to the lace heading (see the photo above). If you wish, carefully trim the fabric from behind the lace, as I did on the blouse on pp. 52-53. Always stitch a test sample and adjust settings.

The sample at right shows the stages of hemstitching insertion laces using the second method. From left to right:
1. The lace is straight-stitched in place.
2. The fabric behind the lace is cut (photo below right) and pressed to the sides.
3. Parisian hemstitching is worked along the folded edges.
4. Excess fabric on the back is trimmed away.

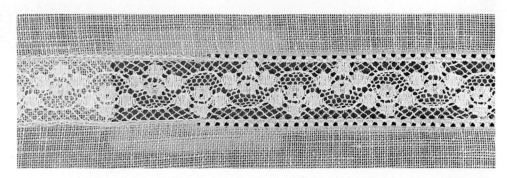

With the second method, after you have straight-stitched the lace in place (the photos above illustrate the process):

1. Carefully cut down the center of the fabric behind the lace.

2. Press each side back toward the fabric along the stitching line.

3. Parisian hemstitch so that the forward and reverse stitches are on the fabric close to the fold, and the stitch to the side goes just over the fold and into the lace.

4. Trim the excess fabric from the back.

Edging laces Edging laces have one straight side (the heading) and one scalloped side. They are applied, either flat or gathered, on an outside edge, for example on collar edges or on any ruffled edges.

To attach edging laces using the first method:

1. With right sides up, straight-stitch (length 2mm) the lace heading to the fabric about ½ in. from the fabric edge. Use a regular needle and basic sewing foot.

2. Switch to the desired hemstitch needle. Hemstitch so that the large holes in the fabric are next to the lace heading and one side of the stitch is just over the heading.

3. Carefully trim the excess fabric from behind the lace. (A sample is shown in the top photo on the facing page.)

For hemstitching edging laces using the first method, the lace is straight-stitched in place, then hemstitched. This sample shows Parisian hemstitching (right) and Venetian hemstitching (left). The fabric behind the lace is trimmed away afterwards, as at left.

Most good-quality laces have threads in the heading that can be pulled for gathering. If the lace does not have a pull thread, stitch one or two rows of slightly lengthened straight stitching (length about 3mm) along the heading. Do not starch lace that is to be gathered.

To attach gathered lace, the first method is usually best:
1. Pull one or two gathering threads in the heading to gather the first few inches of the lace. Do not gather lace too fully except where it is to be attached to sharp curves or corners.
2. Stitch the gathered lace onto the fabric in the desired position with a straight stitch (length 2mm) or tiny zigzag stitch (width 1mm, length 1.5mm) along the heading, gathering the lace as you go. Use a regular needle (size 70) and basic sewing foot. (If the gathered heading is bulky, use a satin-stitch foot.)
3. Switch to the desired hemstitch needle and hemstitch with one side of the hemstitch on the fabric and the other side over the lace heading. Both the Parisian and Venetian stitches work well (a sample is shown in the photo at right). The large holes will be in the fabric right next to the lace heading. Always stitch a test sample and adjust settings.
4. Carefully trim the fabric from behind the lace.

To attach edging laces using the second method:
1. Position the lace and fabric right sides together, so that the scalloped edge of the lace faces away from the fabric edge and the heading is about ½ in. from the fabric edge. Straight-stitch the lace heading to the fabric using a regular needle and basic sewing foot.
2. Press the seam allowance (the ½ in. of fabric along the edge) toward the wrong side of the fabric along the seam line so that the scalloped edge of the

T I P

On collars and pinafore-style bibs that are to be lined, the seam attaching the garment to the lining may be eliminated by hemstitching the gathered lace to both layers, as was done on the bib in the photo at left on p. 92. Cording the hemstitching will add stability and strength, but this technique is not recommended for loosely woven fabrics.

Gathered lace is first stitched in place, then hemstitched along the heading. This sample shows Parisian hemstitching (right) and Venetian hemstitching (left). The fabric has been trimmed behind the portion at left.

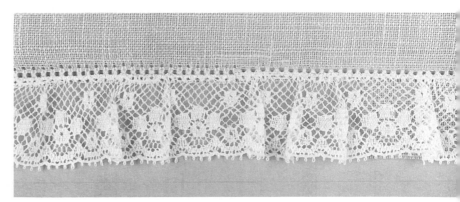

For hemstitching edging laces with the second method, the lace heading is straight-stitched about ½ in. from the fabric edge (right sides together) with the scallops away from the fabric edge (right). Then the seam allowance is pressed toward the wrong side of the fabric with the lace extending (left).

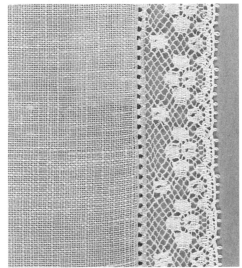

The pinafore-style bib (center) is embellished with lace insertion and gathered edging sewn with the Venetian hemstitch, as well as with corded pintucks. The square collar on the dresser has tatted edging attached with the Venetian hemstitch, ribbon appliquéd with the Parisian hemstitch, and rows of Turkish hemstitching. On the spoke collar in the drawer, lace insertion and edgings were attached with the Parisian hemstitch.

In this sample of the second method, Parisian hemstitching was worked over the lace heading and the folded edge of fabric. The excess fabric has been trimmed from the back.

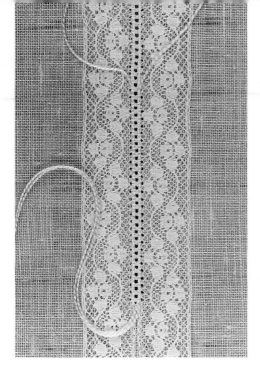

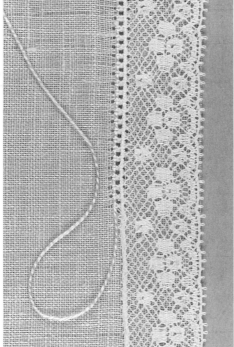

Two side-by side adjoining laces can be hem-stitched using the Venetian stitch. In the center section of the sample the stitch has been corded.

Cording the hemstitches for attaching lace to fabric (center of sample) adds stability and a fin-ished appearance.

T I P

If the lace heading itself is cordlike, it is not nec-essary to cord the side of the stitch that goes over it. For example, to Venetian hemstitch such a lace to fabric, cord would be needed only on the side of the stitch that goes into the fabric (see the photo at near left). To Venetian hem-stitch two insertions with cordlike headings side by side, additional cord may not be needed at all. Likewise, the gathered heading of laces may be thick enough to have the same raised effect as cord.

lace extends from the fabric, as shown in the top right photo on the facing page.
3. Switch to a hemstitch needle and with right side up, Parisian hemstitch so that the large holes are in the fabric near the folded edge and the stitch to the side goes just over the folded edge and into the lace. Trim the excess fabric from the back. (A sample is shown in the photo at bottom right on the facing page.)

Side-by-side adjoining laces

Use the technique described here for attaching two side-by-side lace inser-tions (as seen on the front of the pinafore-style bib in the photo at left on the facing page) or an insertion and an adjoining edging to fabric. Arrange the laces so that their designs meet in a pleasing way.

1. Spray-starch and press the laces as straight as possible, without stretching.
2. Stitch one lace insertion onto the fabric in the desired position with a straight stitch (length 2 mm) or tiny zigzag (width 1mm, length 1.5mm) along both headings. Use a regular needle (size 70) and basic sewing foot. Do not straight-stitch the other lace in place in case you need to adjust the spacing between the laces.
3. Switch to the desired hemstitch needle and, if necessary, a satin-stitch foot. Stitch the Venetian hemstitch between the two lace headings so that one side of the stitch goes over one heading and the other side goes over the other heading, stitching it in place (see the photo above left). Always stitch a test sample to determine exactly how far apart the headings should be.

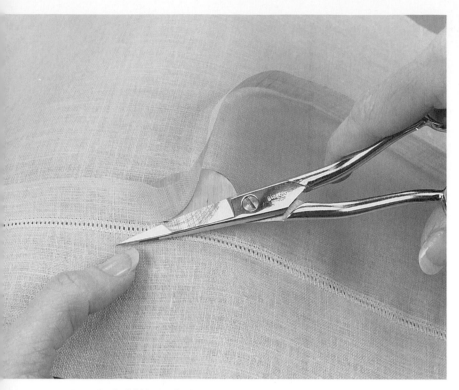

On a single-fold hem, the hemstitching is done from the right side, then excess fabric is trimmed from the wrong side. This method is good for sheer fabrics.

If you don't have the Venetian hemstitch, use the Parisian hemstitch between the laces, with the stitch to the side catching the heading of one lace. Then pivot the fabric and stitch the second pass, hitting the same holes between the laces and letting the stitch to the side catch the other heading.

If you wish, carefully trim the fabric from behind the lace.

Attaching lace with corded hemstitches
Hemstitches attaching lace can also be corded. The cord creates a more raised and finished appearance and also adds stability. In general, the cord(s) should be directly over the lace heading(s). A presser foot with holes or grooves to guide the cord is ideal. (Cords, presser feet, and cording different stitches are discussed on pp. 76-79.) With Venetian hemstitch you can stitch over two cords and lace headings at one time, creating the look of lace joined with entredeux.

HEMMING

You can use hemstitching to put in a hem or to topstitch over a skirt, sleeve, or square collar hem. There are two basic methods to hem with hemstitching. One involves hemstitching through the garment and a single-fold hem. The other involves Parisian hemstitching the traditional double-fold hem. Either method works well to hide a crease line when you are letting a hem down.

Single-fold hemstitched hem For the single-fold hem any of the hemstitching methods and stitches, as well as cording, can be used. It is a great way to hem sheer fabrics where a traditional hem would be unattractive (see the photo on p. 80). Shaped hems, where the lower hem edge is straight and the stitched edge of the hem is shaped, for example in large scallops, are especially easy to do with this method.
1. Press the hem with the raw edge to the wrong side.
2. Hemstitch from the right side so that the stitching is at least ¼ in. from the raw edge of the hem allowance underneath.
3. Trim the excess hem-allowance fabric to the hemstitching, as shown in the photo above left.

Double-fold hemstitched hem For the traditional double-fold hem, the Parisian hemstitch is preferred, although other hemstitches can be used. The Parisian hemstitch is easy to do and gives the look of an elegant hand pin-stitched hem (see the top photo on the facing page).
1. Press the raw edge of the hem allowance under about ⅜ in., then pin the hem in place.
2. Since the Parisian hemstitch often looks the same from either side, you can usually stitch this hem wrong side up, as

The Parisian hemstitch gives texture and definition to the bands of facing and sleeve hems of this purchased linen blouse. The single layer of fabric is pierced by the forward and reverse stitches; the facing bands and the double-fold hems are caught by the side stitches.

The Parisian stitch is a good choice for hemstitching a double-fold hem. It can usually be stitched from the wrong side. The forward and reverse stitches are right next to the hem, and the stitch to the side catches the hem.

shown in the photo at right. Stitch a sample to test. The forward and reverse stitches should be on the single layer of the garment close to the hem. The stitch to the side should be just wide enough to catch the hem. An adjustable blind hem or similar foot will help with guiding. If necessary, use a basic zigzag foot. Guide the fold just left of center, in most cases.

If you wish to cord the stitch, or if the stitch looks better from the right side:
1. Straight-stitch the hem in place from the wrong side close to the turned-under

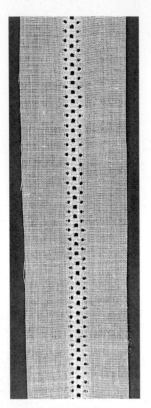

Purchased entredeux? No, this is the Venetian hemstitch corded with buttonhole twist/topstitching thread.

edge. Use fine thread, a regular needle, and normal stitch length (about 2mm). 2. Hemstitch (over cord, if you wish) from the right side so that the stitch to the side goes into the hem, and the forward and reverse stitches creating the large holes are in the single layer of fabric next to the hem. (Use a 120 Universal or other large needle for hemstitching.) The line of straight stitches acts as a guide and usually will be covered by the cord or disguised by the stitching so that removal is not necessary. However, if the straight stitching shows too much on your test sample, stitch it a little farther from the turned-under edge, using a stitch length of about 3mm and a slightly loosened upper tension. Use the stitching as a guide, then remove it.

Additional applications for hemstitching include stitching a narrow hem and hemstitching at the same time (see p. 140) and cording Venetian hemstitch to create fagoting that resembles entredeux (see pp. 110-113).

Questions

I want to purchase a sewing machine with the Parisian hemstitch (pin stitch) and the Venetian hemstitch. Is there a moderately priced machine with these stitches?

These stitches are most often included on the mid-range to top-of-the-line machines. Check the chart on pp. 147-148 for machines with these stitches. If the current models are out of your price range (remember to inquire about sales), ask the dealer about good used machines.

For hemstitching on the sewing machine, must a new wing needle be used for every garment?

That depends. There are many factors to consider. Some garments have only one row of hemstitching, while others have numerous rows. Some hemstitches have seven stitches in the stitch pattern while others have thirteen. Sometimes a tearaway stabilizer is needed under the fabric being hemstitched, and this will dull a needle faster. (Before lightweight tearaway products became available, paper sometimes had to be used to stabilize hemstitching. It was not uncommon to have to use more than one needle per garment.)

On a special project, if there is any doubt, use a new needle. You may also want to experiment with size 120/19 Universal needles for hemstitching. On many fabrics I like these better than a wing needle, and a package of five Universal needles costs about the same as one wing needle.

Is it possible to make entredeux on the sewing machine?

The corded Venetian hemstitch can look remarkably like entredeux (see the photo above left). But why make entredeux on a strip of fabric, only to have to trim it and zigzag it to lace or fabric, when you can do it all in one step? Cord the Venetian hemstitch when using it for any of the applications described in this chapter and you will have the look of entredeux without the additional steps and seam allowances.

In the rare event that you do need to make the entredeux separately (for example, if the garment fabric is not appropriate for hemstitching), follow the instructions for corded Venetian hemstitch on p. 78. Use fine machine-embroidery cotton thread, such as Madeira size 80 or Mettler size 60/2. Use

Topstitching with the Parisian hemstitch adds a subtle accent to the collar and tucks on a simple white blouse. The double-fold sleeve hems are hemmed and hemstitched in one step using the same stitch.

size 8 pearl cotton or topstitching thread/buttonhole twist for the cord.

Good-quality purchased entredeux comes on a strip of Swiss batiste. But since all, or at least most, of the fabric is trimmed after it is applied, you can substitute a similar fabric such as a pima cotton batiste. Stitching crossgrain (selvage to selvage) is always easiest. If you need a longer length than the fabric width allows, remove the selvages and overlap the fabric by about ¼ in. Another option is to piece stitched lengths together, overlapping one or two holes when applying it, the same way entredeux is pieced.

Put a lightweight tearaway stabilizer under the fabric. Tear it away gently after stitching. A size 100 wing needle will create good-size holes, but is hard on the fabric. For a more delicate look, like that of baby entredeux, try a 120/19 Universal needle. The automatic stitch settings on most machines are too wide and long. Narrow and shorten them to approximate the size of entredeux.

I have not been able to get good results using a wing needle to hemstitch lace onto polyester/cotton batiste dresses for my daughter. My attempts at hemstitching down the front of a polyester/cotton (65% polyester, 35% cotton) broadcloth blouse for myself look terrible. Help!
It is the polyester in both these fabrics that makes your hemstitching problematic. It is very difficult to hemstitch polyester/cotton broadcloth, especially lengthwise (parallel to the selvage), without getting unsightly puckering. Try the following recommendations for hemstitching any difficult fabric:
• Avoid hemstitching long lengthwise rows. Consider using just touches of crossgrain hemstitching instead. For example, on a girl's batiste dress, hemstitch lace to the edge of smocked or gathered sleeves and possibly to the collar. On your blouse, hemstitch the collar and possibly the pocket or, if it is short sleeved, hem the sleeves with hemstitching.
• Prewash broadcloth or other fabrics where sizing on the surface could be a factor. Stabilize the fabric. First try multiple applications of spray starching and pressing. If the test samples still pucker, use a lightweight tearaway stabilizer under the fabric. After stitching, tear it away very gently.
• Use a new, good-quality Universal needle. A wing needle usually causes puckering on fabrics other than loosely woven cottons and linens. Use the smallest size that will give the desired effect. (Remember that for the stitching to resemble hand pin stitching, the holes should be only slightly enlarged.)
• Use fine machine-embroidery cotton thread, such as Madeira size 80 or Mettler size 60/2.
• Use a simpler hemstitch, such as the Parisian hemstitch, with fewer stitches in its pattern.
• Use a short stitch length and a narrow width.
• Try a basic metal zigzag presser foot to hold the fabric more securely. If a satin-stitch foot is needed, a metal one will hold better than a plastic one.
• Stitch at a smooth, even slow to medium speed.
• Try cording the hemstitching. It adds stability.
• If there is puckering, loosen upper tension (i.e. adjust to a lower number). If the stitches are too loose, tighten upper tension only as much as absolutely necessary.

Always stitch a test sample with conditions the same as on the garment, including grain direction and stabilizer. If you try all these tips and there is still unsightly puckering, the best solution may be to change either the embellishment or the fabric. Because of its tight weave, 100% cotton (pima or pinpoint cotton) broadcloth is not as easy to hemstitch as linen, but it is much easier than polyester/cotton broadcloth.

Chambray (the one used for the blouse on p. 97 is 80% cotton/20% polyester and comes in white and pastel colors), Swiss cotton piqué, and, of course, other fabrics with a high percentage of linen or cotton are all good choices.

The simplicity of this purchased ramie blouse is enhanced with just a hint of embellishment—a Parisian hemstitch decorates the facing bands at the edges of the neck and sleeve.

6

Fagoting

A navy linen blouse gets a classic finish. The pocket and sleeves of this purchased garment were cut; the edges were folded and finished with a corded edge, then joined with briar-stitch fagoting. The pintuck foot makes easy work of guiding the corded edges for the fagoting.

Feather and briar variations

Honeycomb

Cross stitch and herringbone variations

Overcasting or multiple zigzag

Block capital letter "I"

Venetian hemstitch

Many of the stitches on your sewing machine may be used for fagoting, a decorative technique used to join fabric or lace. With fagoting, space for decorative stitching is purposely left between the two pieces being joined. You can use fagoting to join two pieces of folded or finished fabric, or to join fabric to lace or lace to lace to create a look amazingly like hand-stitched fagoting (and without all the latter's basting and marking!). It is a beautiful effect that gives a classic, handsewn look to blouse fronts, yokes, sleeves, collars, lingerie, pinafore bibs or aprons, and table or bed linens. And it is also a decorative way to lengthen a dress or skirt. The sidebar on p. 105 suggests ways to use this technique to embellish your garments.

Fagoting fabric to fabric

Specifications for machine fagoting to join two fabrics are as follows:

Fabric: Usually light- to medium-weight wovens, but almost any fabric with body or fabric that can be spray-starched and pressed to give it body. Always test on scraps first.

Thread: Cotton, or for more shine, rayon. Experiment with other decorative threads. Thread size is determined by the look desired. For more visibility, thread two threads through the needle, or wind heavier thread or cord onto the bobbin and sew with the right side of the fabric down. Thread color may match or contrast with the fabric color.

Needle: Appropriate for fabric and thread being used, most often 80 Universal.

Foot: Basic metal zigzag foot. A pin-tuck or other foot can be substituted if it has grooves or markings that would be helpful for guiding the fabric edges, as

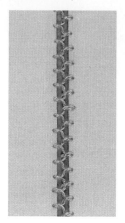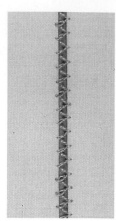

The sample at left shows fagoting with a feather, or briar, stitch. The one at right is a honeycomb stitch (which looks very different stitched across space than it does on fabric).

long as the presser foot holds the pieces being joined securely over the feed dogs.

Stitch: Many stitches can be used for machine fagoting, including:
- feather and briar variations,
- honeycomb,
- cross stitch and herringbone variations,
- overcasting or multiple zigzag,
- block capital letter "I"
- Venetian hemstitch.

Experiment with other stitches. With cord on the bobbin, choose less dense stitches, such as the multiple zigzag.

Width: 4mm to 6mm (or wider). Note: Stitch numbers and settings for some machines are listed on pp. 147-148.

Length: Varies with stitch used and look desired; most common range is 1.5mm to 2.5mm.

Tension: Loosened upper tension; normal bobbin tension usually. (With cord on bobbin: upper tension normal to tightened; bobbin tension loosened or bypassed.)

Accessories: Flat coffee stirrer (for Elnas, the fagoting plate). Slide-on sewing table for larger work surface, if your machine has one.

Always stitch practice samples first. Fold under about 1 to 1½ in. on the two pieces of fabric. (For metric conversion, see the chart on p. 30.) Spray-starch and press several times; giving the fabric body helps prevent puckering and rippling. Hold the two folded edges parallel about ⅛ in. to 3/16 in. apart and begin to stitch. The stitch should go into one folded edge, then "in the air" (across the space between the two fabrics), and into the other folded edge.

Adjust the space between the fabrics on your practice piece according to the stitch width. The stitches should look the same on both fabrics. If only one stitch is being taken on one fold, and three stitches are being taken on the other fold, adjust your guiding so that the same number of stitches will be taken on each side. (In most cases, this will be one stitch.) Stitch slowly, with an even rhythm.

GUIDING AIDS

You can guide the two edges along markings on a presser foot or the needle plate on some machines. (For example, the two red lines on foot 0A on Pfaff models 1469, 1471, 1473, 1475, and possibly others, are perfect fagoting guides with briar stitch #29, set at width 6mm, length 2.5mm.)

Elna has wide and narrow fagoting plates that snap onto the needle plate of many of their models to help maintain an even distance between the two pieces. (On the computerized Elnas with wider stitch-width capability, I prefer the wide fagoting plate.)

A flat coffee stirrer taped directly in front of the presser foot (or in front of the fagoting plate on Elnas) makes a useful long guide for fagoting (see the photo below). Simply guide the folded edges of the fabric along each side of the stirrer. Since not all stitches are exactly centered, test to find the best placement for the stirrer. Stirrers come in slightly different widths for greater or less distance between the pieces. Look for suitable ones when you get coffee to go!

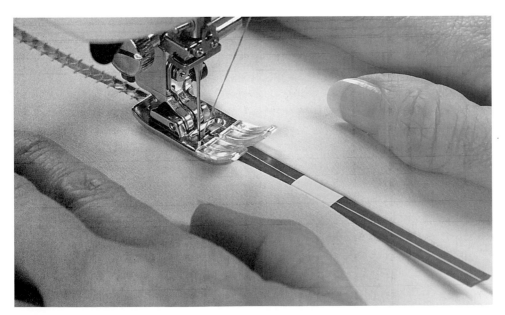

A flat coffee stirrer taped in front of the presser foot makes an effective long guide for fagoting. The folded edges of the fabric are guided along each side of the stirrer.

TIP

For machines that stitch only up to 4mm or 5mm wide, you can trim a plastic coffee stirrer to make it narrower, if necessary.

Guiding for fagoting is much easier when the fabric edges have been corded first. With a five- or seven-groove pintuck foot, you can guide the corded edges into grooves right and left of center.

TIP

To finish a doubled layer of fabric, as was done on the lower sleeve and upper pocket on the blouse in the photo on pp. 100-101 and the upper pocket on the blouse in the photo on p. 106, press the fold line, open flat, and straight-stitch the two layers together along this creased line. Then re-press the fold and zigzag over cord along it.

FAGOTING CORDED EDGES

If you find guiding tedious even with the guiding aids, try fagoting corded edges. First cord each folded fabric edge by zigzagging over cord (see pp. 44-45). The cord and thread color may match or contrast with the fabric. The cord size should be appropriate for the fabric and the look desired. (For example, use relatively small size 8 pearl cotton for a delicate look on lightweight fabrics.) Make the zigzag just wide enough for the stitch to "bite" securely into the folded fabric (a stitch width of about 2mm to 2.5mm); the length should be a little longer than a satin stitch (about .8mm).

For fagoting, position the corded edges under a five- or seven-groove pintuck foot so that the cord rides in the grooves right and left of center. This will make guiding much easier. Adjust the stitch width so the stitches go just into the fabric on each side, as shown in the photo above. Because of the zigzag stitch for the cording, you can trim the fabric up to the stitching on the underside.

ALTERNATIVE METHODS

The method described above produces fagoting that looks the most like hand-stitched, but there are other ways to achieve the look of fagoted fabric to fabric on your sewing machine. Some of these involve stitching two flat pieces of fabric right sides together with a very loose stitch; the fabrics are then folded back along the stitching and pressed. The loose stitch (usually a zigzag stitched over a looping, fringe, or tailor-tack foot) allows space to be left between the two folded edges. The threads between the two sides may be bundled by hand with a needle and thread. Viking has a hemstitch fork that goes between the two fabrics. The fabrics are stitched with a loose, long

Using fagoting on a garment

Fagoting and other decorative work should be done before the pattern piece is cut out. The garment must be planned to include a way to finish the raw edge under each fold. Since fagoting is often used on garments with a handsewn look, the fabric may be sheer. With sheer fabrics simply overcasting the pressed-under edges is often unacceptable because this would show through the fabric.

Here are some creative but easy ways to finish the raw edges under the folds. (Keep in mind that, unless the fabric is very loosely woven, you can safely trim up to a medium to wide zigzag stitch and its variations.)

• Hemstitch through both layers an attractive distance from the fold, then trim away the excess fabric on the underside up to the hemstitching.

• Stitch a dense decorative stitch, such as a scallop (other than the tracery scallop, which is not dense) through both layers, then trim, as was done on the front of the blouse in the photo on pp. 26-27.

• Use twin needles and a decorative stitch such as a tracery scallop to stitch through both layers, then trim (see the photo at right). The bobbin thread zigzags with twin-needle stitching, so that the excess fabric may be trimmed up to the stitching on the underside. The decorative stitch can "frame" the fagoting for the effect of embroidered insertion.

• Use twin needles with a straight stitch, catch both layers in pintucks, then trim.

• Plan the garment so that both layers extend to the outer edge of the project. The edges will be caught in the seams or attached to the edging. This method in effect gives the piece a lining, and is suitable for small pieces such as a pinafore bib, yoke or a square collar.

• Zigzag over cord along the folded edges (see "Fagoting corded edges" on the facing page). Use a pintuck foot for fagoting, then trim away the fabric up to the stitching on the underside.

• Hide the raw edge in a folded tuck (see the photos below). This was done on the sleeves of the blouse on pp. 26-27.

• Stitch the fagoting on narrow or rolled hem edges (as long as the stitching or bulk of the hem does not detract from the fagoting).

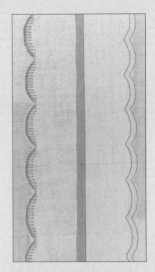

Scallops (a dense decorative scallop on the left and twin-needle tracery scallops at right) are attractive ways to finish the raw edges under each fold prior to fagoting. In either case the excess fabric on the underside can be trimmed to the stitching.

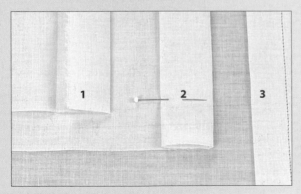

A folded tuck is a practical way to conceal the raw edge under the fold for fagoting.
1. The raw edge is pressed under (1 in. in this sample).
2. The folded edge is turned and pressed again .

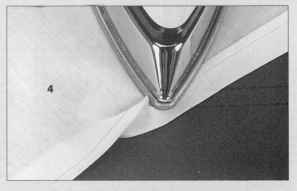

3. The tuck is stitched ¼ in. from the second fold.
4. If the tucks are to frame the fagoting, they should then be opened and pressed away from the edge to be fagoted.

The pocket of this purchased blouse has the look of hand fagoting. The pocket was cut; the edges were folded and corded with contrasting pearl cotton, then joined with the briar (or feather) stitch. The mandarin collar (and cuffs) are outlined with Parisian hemstitching sewn over cording, which frames a decorative machine stitch.

straight stitch between the prongs of the fork; the fork creates distance between the two fabrics so that when the fabrics are pressed open, the loose straight stitches become ladder-like fagoting.

Fagoting lace

Following are specifications for fagoting lace:

Lace: Best with mostly cotton laces that have narrow headings. (A heading is the straight edge on one side of a lace edging and on both sides of a lace insertion.) Very straight laces at least ⅝ in. to ¾ in. wide are easiest to handle, but narrower laces may be used. (Embroideries with entredeux attached and some other trims also work well for fagoting.) The laces should be spray starched and pressed several times, keeping them as straight as possible for straight applications and shaping for curved applications. Take care not to stretch the laces.

Stabilizer: Tearaway or water-soluble stabilizer. With water-soluble stabilizer, press two layers together (between pressing cloths, with medium heat and no steam) to give more body. To fuse fabric and/or lace temporarily in the desired position, lightly spray-starch the wrong side of the fabric or lace, lay it in place over the stabilizer, and press (again with a dry iron and press cloth). After stitching, tear or cut away excess stabilizer; the rest will dissolve with water.

There are two basic problems to deal with when fagoting lace. The first is that because lace is usually so soft and open, it easily gets distorted and pulled. The second is that holding the lace securely is difficult. Both conditions can cause the lace to be pulled out of shape and toward the piece to which it is being joined, closing the desired gap.

Compensate for lace's softness by carefully spray starching and pressing the lace several times until it is stiff. It is important not to stretch the lace. If it is stretched, then spray starched, pressed, and stitched, it will relax with the first washing, causing ripples in your beautiful project.

The easiest way to compensate for the second problem is to choose wider laces. I find that I can adequately hold the outside edge of a lace that is at least ¾ in. wide by using my entire index finger (not just the fingertip) as it passes under the presser foot. For a narrower lace, or any lace that is difficult to hold, attach the lace to stabilizer so that you then have something that is easier to hold. Baste the lace (by machine with loosened upper tension) over a strip of tearaway stabilizer that is about 3 in. wide. Leave about ¼ in. of the lace (the heading plus a little extra) extending beyond the stabilizer so that the stabilizer will not be caught in the fagoting stitches, as shown in the photo on p. 108. The loosened tension makes the basting stitches easy to remove when the stabilizer is no longer needed.

Another option is to fuse the lace temporarily to water-soluble stabilizer. Press two layers of stabilizer together, as explained at left under "Stabilizer." Then *lightly* spray-starch the back of the lace, lay it in place over the stabilizer, and press (with a dry iron and press cloth) to fuse.

Although you can stitch fagoting through water-soluble stabilizer, in most cases I prefer the look of fagoting stitched "in the air," so I usually let the lace heading extend as described for tearaway stabilizer. (The exception to this is "Fagoting with appliqué cord and

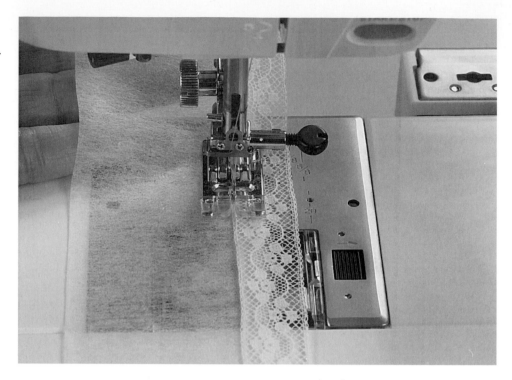

the Venetian hemstitch," discussed on pp. 110-112.) The water-soluble stabilizer can usually be pulled gently from the lace after stitching and can even be reused. If your lace was very damp when it was fused, it will not pull away easily; so trim off the excess stabilizer and dissolve the rest in water.

FAGOTING LACE TO FABRIC

Always stitch practice samples before working on your project. Spray-starch and press the folded fabric and the lace several times. Finish the fabric edge, using one of the suggestions in the sidebar on p. 105 or any finish you prefer. A corded edge, done with a fine cord that matches the fabric, makes an attractive simple finish for fabric being fagoted to lace (see the top photo on the facing page). Unless the lace is wide enough to be held securely, baste it to tearaway stabilizer or temporarily fuse it to a water-soluble stabilizer.

Hold the fabric fold and the lace heading parallel about ⅛ in. to ³⁄₁₆ in. apart and stitch. The stitch should go into the fabric fold, across the space, and then just over the lace heading, catching the heading only (see the bottom photo on the facing page). Adjust the space and the guiding, if necessary. If the two edges are being pulled together, loosen upper tension a little more.

FAGOTING LACE TO LACE

As always, stitch practice samples first. Spray-starch and press the laces several times. If your project requires the other heading of one or both laces to be attached to fabric, this step is best done before the fagoting so that you will not have to attach the lace to stabilizer (see the top photo on the facing page). Otherwise, baste the lace to tearaway stabilizer or temporarily fuse it to a water-soluble stabilizer.

In this detail from a square collar, fagoting joins fabric to lace and lace to lace. The folded edge of the Swiss batiste fabric was finished with a fine corded edge. The first lace insertion was fagoted to the corded edge, then each additional lace was added.

Hold the two lace headings parallel about ⅛ in. to ³⁄₁₆ in. apart and stitch. The stitch should go just over one lace heading, across the space between the laces, and then just over the other lace heading. Catch only the headings with the stitches. Adjust the spacing, guiding, and tension, if necessary.

You may also want to test stitching through water-soluble stabilizer to see which method you prefer. If so, fuse one lace near the center of two fused sheets of water-soluble stabilizer. Lay the other lace about ⅛ in. to ³⁄₁₆ in. from the fused one. Do not fuse this lace in place because you would then have no way to adjust the spacing. Stitch as before. Instead of being "in the air," the stitching between the two laces will go into the stabilizer. After stitching trim the excess stabilizer, then dissolve the rest in water. After the stabilizer has dissolved, the stitching between the laces may stretch; tightening tension slightly may help if the stretching is excessive.

When fagoting lace to fabric, the fabric fold and the lace heading should be parallel and ⅛ in. to ³⁄₁₆ in. apart. Here the lace has been temporarily fused to water-soluble stabilizer (two layers fused together) to make holding the lace easier. A coffee stirrer aids guiding.

Fagoting with appliqué cord and the Venetian hemstitch

Combining appliqué-cord hemstitching with fagoting techniques creates a very finished and strong corded fagoting stitch that very closely resembles entre-deux, a ladder-looking trim used in heirloom sewing as well as on designer ready-to-wear (see the photo below). As with fagoting without cord, you can join fabric to lace, lace to lace, or fabric to fabric using this technique.

Both lace and fabric should be prepared as for other fagoting techniques. The specifications that differ from those for other fagoting are as follows:

Thread: Extra-fine machine-embroidery cotton (Madeira size 80, Mettler size 60, Zwicky size 70, or DMC size 50). Color should match cord color or be a shade lighter.

Cord: Topstitching thread, button-hole twist, cordonnet, or pearl cotton (usually size 8). Cord color should match thread color or be a shade darker.

Needle: Large Universal—120/19, 110/18, 100/16, etc. depending on the fabric chosen and the look desired.

Presser foot: Ideally, foot with holes to guide the cord (such as Bernina's five-groove foot #25, either of Elna's multiple-cord soles, and Pfaff's 7/9 hole or Viking's seven-hole cording foot); or a foot with grooves immediately left and right of center (such as a traditional button-hole foot or Pfaff's foot 1A). If your machine does not have such a foot, perhaps another brand's foot will work on it with the use of an adaptor and/or a different shank. A satin-stitch foot can be used, but guiding the cords will be harder.

Upper tension: Usually normal, but if the holes created between the cords are not distinct, slightly increase upper tension; if there is puckering, slightly decrease upper tension.

Stitch: Venetian hemstitch.

Width: Usually 3mm to 4.5mm. Test.

Length: Varies by machine, but usually the same as for hemstitching with this stitch.

Venetian hemstitch

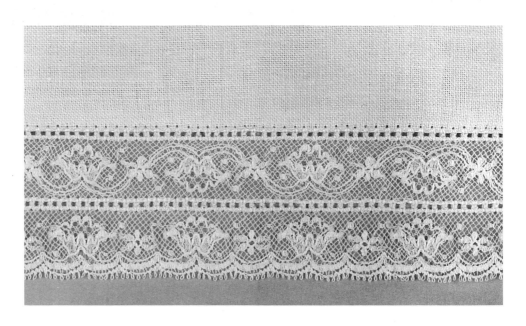

In this sample, the corded Venetian hemstitch was used to fagot an insertion lace to fabric and an edging lace to the other heading of the insertion lace. (It's best to do any lace-to-fabric fagoting before doing the lace-to-lace work, as the fabric gives you something to hold onto.)

FAGOTING LACE TO FABRIC WITH APPLIQUÉ CORD

As always, test on scraps first.

1. Fuse the starched and folded edge of fabric in place over two sheets of water-soluble stabilizer.

2. Position the lace (without fusing) so that the heading is about $\frac{1}{16}$ in. to $\frac{1}{8}$ in. from the folded fabric edge.

3. Stitch with the Venetian hemstitch so that the left side of the stitch just catches the fabric, the right side goes just over the lace heading, and the prominent holes are centered between the lace and the fabric. Adjust the spacing between the fabric and lace, and balance the stitch, if necessary (see the sidebar on p. 74).

4. Stop with the needle down in the center and raise the presser foot.

5. Lay the cords on each side of the needle or, if you are using a cording foot, use a dental-floss threader to thread the cord through the holes just left and right of center (see the photo on p. 76).

6. Lower the presser foot and stitch. The left cord should be just on the fabric fold; the left side of the stitch will now go over it. The right cord will be over the lace heading, and the right side of the stitch will now go over it. The large holes will be centered between the two cords. Slight additional balancing of the stitch may be necessary.

Note: The cord over the folded fabric edge is optional. Remove the left cord and stitch a few inches on the test sample with just the right cord over the lace heading to see which you prefer.

FAGOTING LACE TO LACE WITH APPLIQUÉ CORD

Prepare the laces in the usual way. Fuse one of the laces in the desired position over two fused sheets of water-soluble stabilizer. Lay the other lace heading in position about $\frac{1}{16}$ in. to $\frac{1}{8}$ in. from the fused lace heading.

Stitch with the Venetian hemstitch so that the left side of the stitch goes just over one lace heading, the right side goes just over the other lace heading, and the prominent holes are centered between the two laces, as shown in the photo below. Adjust the spacing between the laces and balance the stitch, if necessary. Stop with the needle down in the center. Add cords, as instructed in steps 5 and 6 at left, so that a cord is over each heading, and stitch.

When fagoting lace to lace using appliqué cord, one lace should be fused to water-soluble stabilizer. The Venetian hemstitch stitches over both cords (and the stabilizer) at the same time. A presser foot with holes to guide the cord is helpful.

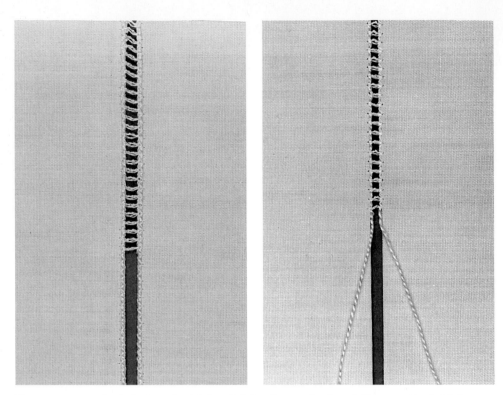

There are two methods for fagoting fabric to fabric using appliqué cord. Either cord both fabric edges first, then stitch the Venetian hemstitch to join them (left) or cord them as you are stitching the Venetian hemstitch (right).

FAGOTING FABRIC TO FABRIC WITH APPLIQUÉ CORD

The technique for fagoting fabric to fabric with appliqué cord is a little different from the technique for lace. There are two ways to do it; samples made with each method are shown in the photos above. With either method, a smaller needle than usual (such as an 80 Universal) will help reduce puckering.

With the first method, the first step is to finish the folded fabric edges with cord (see pp. 44-45). Then stitch the Venetian hemstitch so that the sides of the stitch go just over each corded edge. The spacing of the grooves on pintuck feet may not be helpful with this stitch. Instead, try a standard buttonhole or other foot with two grooves, or a satin-stitch foot plus a guiding aid such as a coffee stirrer. This method is usually

easier than the second method and also looks more finished. With it, you can trim up to the stitching on the underside.

The second method is more like fagoting lace with appliqué cord. If you are using a foot with grooves, lay a cord over each folded edge, and lower the presser foot to align the cords (and fabric edges) with grooves that keep them 1/16 in. to 1/8 in. apart. If you are using a cording foot, use a dental-floss threader to thread cord through holes just left and right of center. Lower the foot so that the left cord is just over the left fabric fold, and the right cord is just over the right fabric fold. Stitch so that the sides of the stitch catch each cord and the folded edge, and the large holes are down the center between the cords.

Questions

I have slightly loosened the upper tension, but the two pieces of fabric are still being pulled together by the fagoting stitches. What else can I do?

First try loosening the upper tension more. Also check that there is nothing along the thread path putting extra resistance on the thread. If there are optional guides at the top of the machine or over the needle, try taking the thread out of them. Be sure to use a stitch that takes multiple steps as it crosses from side to side, such as one of those suggested on p. 102. (A regular zigzag with one wide stitch from side to side pulls the fabrics together.) Use a presser foot that holds the fabric securely, such as the basic metal zigzag foot, and hold the fabrics firmly with your hands as you guide.

If the gap between the fabrics is still disappearing, perhaps your bobbin tension is too tight. Try bypassing or loosening bobbin tension. (If you have a separate bobbin case set for a looser tension for heavier threads, try it.)

Another option is to use a water-soluble stabilizer underneath. Fuse one fabric to the stabilizer. Leave the other unfused so you can adjust the space between them, if necessary. Test carefully because the stitching sometimes stretches when the stabilizer dissolves.

I understand that lace can be attached to fabric using the fagoting with appliqué cord technique (over water-soluble stabilizer) or using the hemstitching appliqué cord technique (over fabric). Both create the look of entredeux. Which is better?

Choosing between the two methods is mostly a matter of personal preference. Hemstitching over fabric is a little easier to do than fusing water-soluble stabilizer. However, you can use a smaller needle with fagoting, so this technique may work better on fabrics unsuitable for hemstitching with a large needle. I would suggest that you stitch a sample of each and see which you like better—for both the look and the process.

7

Hemming and Re-hemming, Plain or Fancy

The feather stitch delicately hems and decorates this little girl's smocked dress, which has a growth tuck hidden on the underside of the hem. The sleeve edges are highlighted with lace attached with the Parisian hemstitch. The ruffles of the blue sundress are finished with 'no-trim-around' scalloped edging.

Hemming is a part of almost every garment you sew. There are times when basic blind hemming is appropriate and times when a more creative treatment is called for. Creative hemming techniques can be used either for their decorative value alone or for solutions to problem hemming situations, such as for hemming sheer fabrics when traditional blind hemming would show through unattractively or for disguising a crease line when lowering a hem.

Blind hemming

With a few tips and a little practice you can blind-hem by machine virtually any garment you would have blind-hemmed by hand, with equally nice results. No one should be able to tell from the right side of the garment that a blind hem was stitched by machine. Blind hemming by machine not only saves time, but also makes the hems more secure than those stitched by hand.

Like most sewers, I was frustrated and disappointed with my first blind hems by machine. Then my daughter Emily started school and wore smocked dresses almost daily. (At the time, I co-owned a shop that specialized in smocking classes and supplies.) There always seemed to be a stack of dresses needing to be hemmed or needing the hems let down, and the hems of most smocked dress are 90 in. around! With practice and refinement (like using finer thread and loosening upper tension), my machine-stitched blind hems became not only acceptable, but almost invisible. Yours can too.

There are two methods for blind hemming. The first is the standard method, where on the wrong side the stitching is about 1/8 in. from the hem's top edge. The second method differs in that some of the stitching is "in the air." The result is that even from the wrong side it's hard to tell the hem was stitched by machine. The photos show the wrong sides of hems stitched each way.

With the standard method of blind hemming (top right), the stitching on the wrong side is about 1/8 in. from the top edge of the hem. With the 'in the air' method (bottom right), it is difficult to tell even from the wrong side that the hem was stitched by machine. (In both samples, contrasting thread was used to make the stitching more visible.)

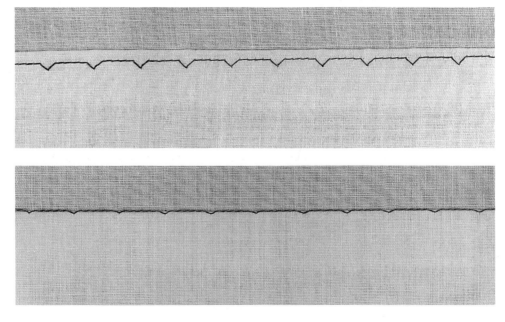

Fabric: Almost any fabric suitable for blind hemming by hand can be blind-hemmed by machine.

Thread: Fine thread is best because the stitches will show less (and thus look more like handsewn)—Coats Dual Duty Plus extra-fine cotton-covered polyester or fine cotton machine-embroidery thread, such as Mettler 60/2, DMC 50, or Madeira No. 50. Coats Dual Duty Plus extra-fine cotton-covered polyester has more strength than the fine all-cotton thread, so it is a good choice if the color you need is available. (Use white on all light pastel fabrics.)

Needle: Use the smallest size appropriate for the fabric and thread being used—most often 70 Universal.

Foot: A blind-hem foot has a guide that helps keep the bite of the stitch into the garment consistent. If the guide is adjustable, start with the vertical guide just to the left of the center mark on the foot.

Stitch: Blind stitch (also called blind hem stitch) for blind hemming woven fabrics.

Some machines also have a stretch blind stitch for hemming knits. The additional zigzags allow more stretch.

If your machine has only one of these stitches, use it for all blind hemming.

Width: Start with the automatic setting or 2.5mm to 3mm, then adjust.

Length: 2mm to 3mm.

Needle position: On some Bernina models, a needle position to the right is necessary. Consult the machine manual or start with the automatic needle-position setting, then adjust if necessary.

Upper tension: Loosen (adjust to a lower number) slightly. (Putting more thread into each stitch helps eliminate puckering and dimpling.) With some blind-hem feet (for example, some Bernina, New Home, and Pfaff blind-hem feet), the stitch to the side goes over a metal wire or finger; loosening tension is less likely to be needed with these.

HEM DEPTH AND CURVED HEMS

The depth of the hem will depend on the bulkiness of the fabric and the shape of the hem, as well as on personal taste. Bulky fabrics and curved hems require a shorter hem depth. The more curve there is, the shorter the hem must be to minimize the extra fullness in the turned-up hem. Circular skirts should be narrow hemmed. (Narrow hemming is covered in Chapter 8.) I find that the majority of girls' garments in light- to medium-weight fabric and on straight grain look nice with 5-in. to 6-in. deep hems. The weight of the hem is attractive, and there is enough hem for letting out as the child grows.

On all curved areas (sometimes only part of the hem, such as the sides, is curved), stitch a row of slightly longer straight stitches about ¼ in. from the edge of the hem for easing in the fullness. Leave long thread tails.

PREPARATION

Finish the lower edge of the garment to prevent raveling. On light- to medium-weight fabrics, press under about ⅜ in. On heavier or thicker fabrics, turning under the edge would create too much bulk. Instead, overcast, serge, cover with seam tape, or enclose the edges in a nylon-tape product such as Seams Great. (When you use seam tape on a curved hem, attach the tape after you have eased in the fullness and pressed.)

Blind stitch

Stretch blind stitch

For blind hemming light- to medium-weight fabrics, press the lower edge of the garment under about ³/₈ in., then measure and pin the hem the desired depth. Place the pins perpendicular to the hem edge with their heads pointing away from the hem, so they can easily be removed as you stitch.

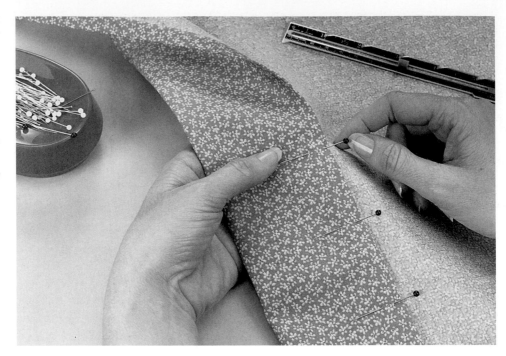

MEASURING, PINNING AND FOLDING

Next, measure and pin the hem the desired depth. Place the pins perpendicular to the hem edge with the heads away from the hem, as shown in the photo above, so that they are easy to remove as you stitch. Draw up the straight stitching as necessary to ease in the fullness of the curved areas. Steam-press the eased areas.

Now take the garment, wrong side out, to the sewing machine. Lay the garment on the machine so that the upper part of the garment is to the left, out of the way. Where you will begin hemming, fold the hem under along the pinned hem edge (specific folding instructions for each method follow). The pins heads will protrude to the right.

STANDARD BLIND HEMMING

When you fold the garment for standard blind hemming, the finished upper edge of the hem should extend approximately ¼ in. to the right, as shown in the top photo on the facing page. Put this ¼-in. hem extension under the blind-hem foot with the garment fold against the guide on the foot (see the bottom photo on the facing page).

Start stitching at a slow speed. Remove the pins as you reach them. The straight stitches will be on the ¼-in. hem extension. When the needle swings to the left to make the wide zigzag, it should barely catch the garment fold so that these stitches will be almost invisible from the right side. If too much of the garment is being caught, adjust by decreasing the stitch width (or with an adjustable foot, by moving the guide to the left). If the zigzag totally misses the garment, widen the stitch (or with an adjustable foot,

At the machine, the garment will be wrong side out, with the hem to the right. Fold the hem under to the right side of the garment along the pinned edge. For the standard blind hem, the top edge of the hem extends about ¼ in.

move the guide to the right). Once the settings are adjusted satisfactorily, use the guide on the foot to feed evenly.

"IN-THE-AIR" BLIND HEMMING

The standard method of blind hemming by machine is more secure and is usually easier to stitch than the "in-the-air" method. The advantage of "in-the-air" blind hemming is that, even on the wrong side, it is difficult to tell that the garment was hemmed by machine.

With this method, the straight stitches are "in the air"—they do not go into fabric at all—and the left swing of the zigzag catches the garment fold and the hem at the same time.

Instructions for this method usually indicate that when the garment is folded for hemming, the hem edge and the fold of the garment should be even. The problem with this arrangement is that, since the zigzag should barely catch the garment, it is too easy for the stitch to miss the hem entirely, creating gaps where the hem is not secured at all. To

With the guide on the blind-hem foot against the garment fold and the top edge of the hem extending to the right, stitch so that the straight stitches are on the hem extension and the zigzag stitches just catch the garment fold.

For 'in-the-air' blind hemming, the hem edge should extend just enough to be seen (less than ¹⁄₁₆ in., but exaggerated here and in the photo above right for clarity), so that when the zigzag catches the garment, it cannot miss the hem.

With the guide of the blind-hem foot against the garment fold, the straight stitches are 'in the air' and the zigzag stitches catch both the garment fold and the hem at the same time. Taut sewing may be necessary.

TIPS

If possible, practice on a scrap before hemming the garment so that you can adjust width and tension. If there is puckering, loosen upper tension.

Start hemming at the back of the garment so that any further adjusting will have been done by the time you get to the front.

correct this potential problem, extend the hem edge just enough to be seen (less than ¹⁄₁₆ in.), as shown in the photo above left. This way, when the zigzag catches the garment, it cannot miss the hem.

Since the stitches are "in the air," there is a tendency for the stitching to draw up. Compensate by loosening the upper tension a little more and holding the fabric taut in front of and behind the presser foot as you stitch, as shown in the photo above right.

Do not be concerned if you or your machine have trouble with the "in-the-air" method. Some machines do not like stitching "in the air." If you can machine-stitch a hem with either method that is almost invisible on the right side of the garment, you have a very usable skill.

Like most skills, blind hemming gets easier and better with practice; so make yourself use it. Start by hemming prints or other fabrics where the stitches will not show so much. Your skill will improve, and soon you will be able to

blind-hem almost anything on your sewing machine and no one else will know it was not done by hand.

PRESSING

After you have stitched the hem, press it flat. If you may eventually let down the hem (as with garments for children), do not press the crease at the lower edge unless necessary, for example, to press in pleats.

Lengthening a hem

It often seems that no sooner do you get a child's garment hemmed, than the child hits a spurt of growth and the garment is too short. Occasionally ladies' dresses and skirts also need lengthening to accommodate changes in style or taste. Simply lowering the hemline is often unacceptable because the original crease line would show too much. When this is the case, you can creatively hide or disguise the crease line. The method you choose must be appropriate for the garment and should look as though it

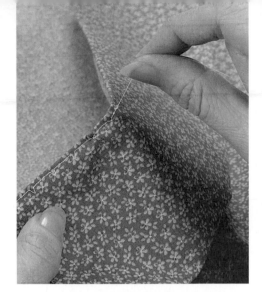

To remove blind-hem stitching in preparation for re-hemming, pull the thread visible on the wrong side of the garment (the bobbin thread).

(the thread visible on the wrong side of the garment), as shown in the photo at left. Flatten the crease left from the original hem by spray starching (if appropriate for the fabric) and pressing it. If the original hem edge was turned under ⅜ in., leave the edge as is if you plan to lower the hem halfway and re-hem the double-fold hem with either the blind stitch for an invisible hem, or for a more decorative hem, the Parisian hemstitch, the feather stitch, or another similar stitch. For most other decorative hemming techniques, unfold and press the edge flat.

The original crease line is most easily concealed if the hem is lowered exactly halfway down. That way the folded (or finished) edge of the hem meets the crease line and helps camouflage it, and the new stitching line along the crease will further disguise it. The drawings below show how. If the crease does not look worn or folded, you can restitch the hem with the traditional blind stitch, or you can use the Parisian hemstitch or the feather stitch to catch the folded

was part of the original garment design, rather than an afterthought.

To prepare for re-hemming, first remove the original hem's stitching. Remove machine blind-hem stitching by pulling what was the bobbin thread

LETTING DOWN A HEM

Letting down a hem exactly halfway helps conceal the crease line of the original hem.

To re-hem with a double-fold hem, leave the hem edge turned under.

To re-hem with a decorative technique stitched from the right side through both fabric layers, press open the turned-under edge.

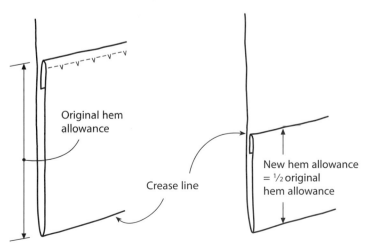

Original hem allowance

Crease line

New hem allowance = ½ original hem allowance

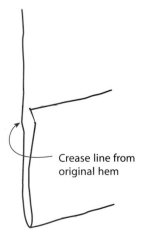

Crease line from original hem

Decorative stitching is difficult to remove. If future lengthening may be needed, consider planning ahead by adding a growth tuck or two (these are folded tucks designed to let out later on for adding length). Another option is to stitch a hidden growth tuck on the underside of the hem, as was done on the baby dress shown in the photo on pp. 114-115.

hem. A crease line that does look worn can be concealed with fagoting, or with decorative stitching over a single-fold hem. It can also be covered with a ribbon or trim, or hidden in a folded tuck, as described below.

Decorative hemming and re-hemming

Hemming offers perfect opportunities to use decorative stitches and techniques. Many of the techniques featured throughout this book can be adapted for creative hemming. For other options, see the sidebar on p. 125.

HEMSTITCHING

If the fabric is appropriate (i.e., mostly cotton or linen), hemstitching is an attractive way to hem or re-hem a garment. You can either hemstitch from the right side through both the garment and single-fold hem and then trim the excess fabric, or you can Parisian hemstitch from the wrong side over a folded hem edge. In the latter case, the large holes are on the single layer of the garment and the stitch to the side catches the folded edge of the hem. (For more information on hemming with hemstitching, see pp. 94-96.) When you are re-hemming a garment, let the hem down halfway and hemstitch over the crease line using either hemstitching method.

TWIN-NEEDLE PINTUCKS

You can hem or re-hem with several rows of twin-needle pintucks stitched from the right side through both layers of fabric (garment and hem). The photo on p. 54 shows an example. If you are re-hemming, let down the hem approximately halfway and stitch one of the rows directly over the original crease. Increase upper tension for a more raised

effect. Cording the pintucks will also create more of a ridge; if the fabric is sheer, the cord can be used to show a shadow of color. On the underside, trim away the excess fabric above the stitching (see pp. 57-60 and p. 63).

TWIN-NEEDLE DECORATIVE STITCHING

Decorative stitches have a new look when stitched with twin needles. Experiment with twin needles and the stitches on your machine to find effects you like. For hemming or re-hemming, the stitch chosen must be appropriate for the garment or it will make the garment look homemade. Stitch from the right side of the garment through both layers (over the crease line if you are re-hemming). To avoid breaking expensive twin needles, test the stitch width very carefully. Slightly loosen upper tension. A lightweight tearaway stabilizer under the fabrics (except for sheers) will reduce tunneling. On sheer fabrics you can create a shadow-work effect with the stitching. Before stitching, give soft sheers body by spray starching and pressing; several applications may be necessary. Trim excess fabric from above the stitching (see pp. 60-63).

ATTACHING NARROW RIBBON WITH TWIN NEEDLES

Another decorative hemming technique is to attach a narrow ribbon using twin needles, stitching from the right side through both layers of the fabric to hem and attach the ribbon at the same time. The middle photo on p. 63 shows an example. When re-hemming, position the ribbon over the crease. Decrease upper tension to keep the ribbon flat. Trim excess fabric after stitching. You can stitch single or multiple rows of ribbon; multiple rows of ribbon could be different colors.

Ribbon widths vary, but usually 2.0/70 or 80 or 2.5/80 twin needles will stitch both sides of ⅛-in. ribbon simultaneously. Hold the points of the needles over the ribbon to decide which size to buy. Twin needles that are farther apart (4mm) also have larger needles (90 or 100). The larger needles may cause problems such as puckering on satin ribbon, but may work fine on grosgrain ribbon (¼ in.) or on some trims. Test first.

SINGLE-NEEDLE DECORATIVE STITCHING

As with twin-needle decorative stitching, when re-hemming it is important to choose the stitch carefully or it will be obvious that the decorative stitch is being used to cover a crease. Because the feather stitch on many machines looks so much like a handsewn stitch, it is often a good choice for a double-fold hem, as can be seen on the hem of the baby dress in the photo on pp. 114-115). It is beautiful when stitched right above the hem with the stitches to one side catching the folded edge of the hem (see the top photo at right).

On single-fold hems, denser, satin-stitch-type decorative stitches can be stitched from the right side through both the garment and the hem (see the middle photo at right). Slightly loosen upper tension. Stabilizing may be needed: Spray-starch (or use another spray-on or paint-on stiffening product) and press; or on fabrics other than sheers, try a tearaway stabilizer. Always test first. Trim the excess fabric after stitching.

FOLDED TUCKS

Folded tucks (see the bottom photo at right) are attractive and may even be used on velveteen and corduroy. When re-hemming, make the crease line of the original hem the folded edge of one

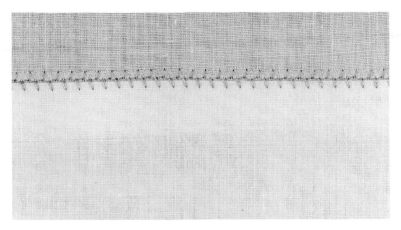

With a single needle and a decorative stitch such as the feather stitch, you can simultaneously stitch a double-fold hem and, if you are re-hemming, conceal the creaseline of the original hem.

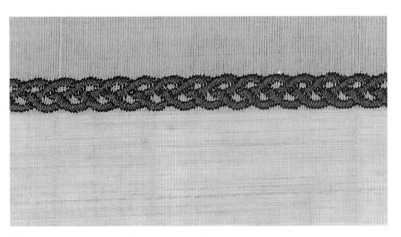

With a dense decorative stitch, you can stitch a single-fold hem.

A folded tuck is a simple but attractive way to re-hem a garment while concealing both the creaseline and the raw edge.

SHELL TUCK

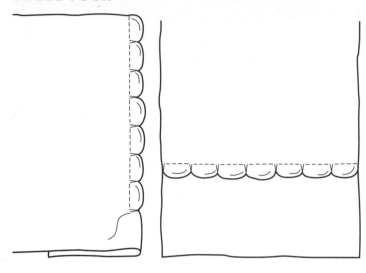

1. Fold fabric as for a regular tuck. Stitch with a satin-stitch foot and blind stitch. The zigzag over the fold creates the shell effect.

2. Open fabric and press tuck in the direction desired. On a skirt this would be down.

TIP

On many fabrics the Parisian hemstitch or feather stitch may be added to embellish the tucks (see p. 87). For feather stitching, first press the tuck. Then center the feather stitch over the straight stitching so that the feathers on one side are on the tuck and those on the other side are just above the tuck (see the organdy pinafore in the photo on p. 56).

tuck. You can conceal the raw edge of the hem in this tuck or in an additional tuck. (See the sidebar on p. 105 for instructions on concealing a raw edge in a folded tuck.) Chapter 2 has tips for precision sewing, including stitching perfect folded tucks.

For a more delicate look on soft, lightweight fabrics, you can use the blind stitch with a satin-stitch foot to stitch one or more rows of small shell tucks. Shell tucks (see the drawing above) are especially appropriate on garments for babies or little girls and for lingerie, such as slips or nightgowns. Fold the fabric as for a regular tuck, but stitch it with the blind stitch rather than a straight stitch. The tuck will be about 3/16 in. deep. In order to create the scalloped effect the stitch to the side must go over the folded edge.

ADDING A TRIM

With a single needle and a straight or zigzag-type stitch (including hem-stitches, if the fabric is appropriate) you can add one or more rows of ribbon or trim, including those too wide for a twin needle. This works well when a hem needs to be let down more than halfway and the crease is above the top of the hem. You can either blind-hem the folded hem edge separately first or catch it in zigzag-type stitching on one side of the trim.

If you are using a zigzag-type stitch to attach the trim, you can stitch from the right side through both the garment and a single-fold hem. Trim the excess hem fabric after stitching. With a lace trim, you can cut away the fabric beneath the lace as well.

FAGOTING

Instead of letting down the original hem, you can simply add to it. Join a folded strip of fabric to the folded crease line with machine fagoting. The strip may be made from the excess fabric in the original hem, if necessary. See p. 105 for ways to finish the raw edges under the folded edges needed for fagoting.

Questions

How much of the garment should be caught in each stitch to the side when blind hemming by machine?
The stitches should be almost invisible from the right side of the garment, which means that the stitch should barely catch the garment. However, there are other considerations that will affect how much the stitch should bite into the fabric, including the wearer, the occasions the garment will be worn, and the type of fabric. For example, on

Other options for lengthening garments

Some garments (including many heirloom garments) may not have been blind-hemmed originally, but may have had a ruffle or other decorative treatment at the lower edge. Options for lengthening these garments may be suitable for garments that were originally blind hemmed as well. These include:

• Inserting a band above the ruffle or hem. The band may include one or more rows of entredeux, lace, embroidery, and so on and be inserted with traditional heirloom techniques, or it may be a plain or embroidered strip of fabric inserted with fagoting.

• Unstitching growth tucks and pintucking the creases. Growth tucks may be let out to lengthen the garment, then twin-needle pintucks may be stitched over any visible crease lines. Additional rows of pin-tucks can be added for a pleasing effect.

• Adding a ruffle. A fabric or eyelet ruffle may be added to a garment that did not have one originally. For some garments an alternative to lengthening the garment itself would be to wear a longer slip with a pretty eyelet ruffle under the garment; it can look as though it was always part of the design.

---

children's play clothes durability is important; so it makes sense to catch a little more than a thread or two of the garment with each stitch. And on prints or loosely woven fabrics, the stitches can be a little wider without being visible than they can on a densely woven solid.

It is always a good idea to stitch a test sample or at least start hemming at the back or in another inconspicuous place to perfect the amount of bite into the garment as well as all other factors. If too much of the garment is being caught, adjust by decreasing the stitch width (or on adjustable blind-hem feet, by moving the guide to the left). Fine thread and slightly loosened tension are also important for the stitches to be almost invisible.

When shortening slacks that taper, how do you hem the narrower lower edge to the wider part of the pant leg above it without getting puckers?
First, avoid making a deep hem on any garment that angles. The more acute the angle, the shallower the hem should be. For slightly tapered slacks, try a 1¼-in. to 1½-in. hem. (Of course, if there is a cuff, the hem must be deeper than the cuff.)

To avoid puckering, the narrower lower edge must be made as wide as the part of the pant leg to which it is being sewn. The easiest way I have found to do this is to open the lower edge of each inseam to about ½ in. from the new hemline, using a seam ripper. If more width is needed, open the seam a little more (to about ¼ in. from the new hemline) and/or open the outside seam. After hemming, secure the seam just below the removed stitches with a few stitches by hand.

For a more professional finish, you can restitch these opened seams to angle out from the hemline to the lower edge. But for most casual slacks I just leave the seam open—because it is at the seam allowance, it does not show.

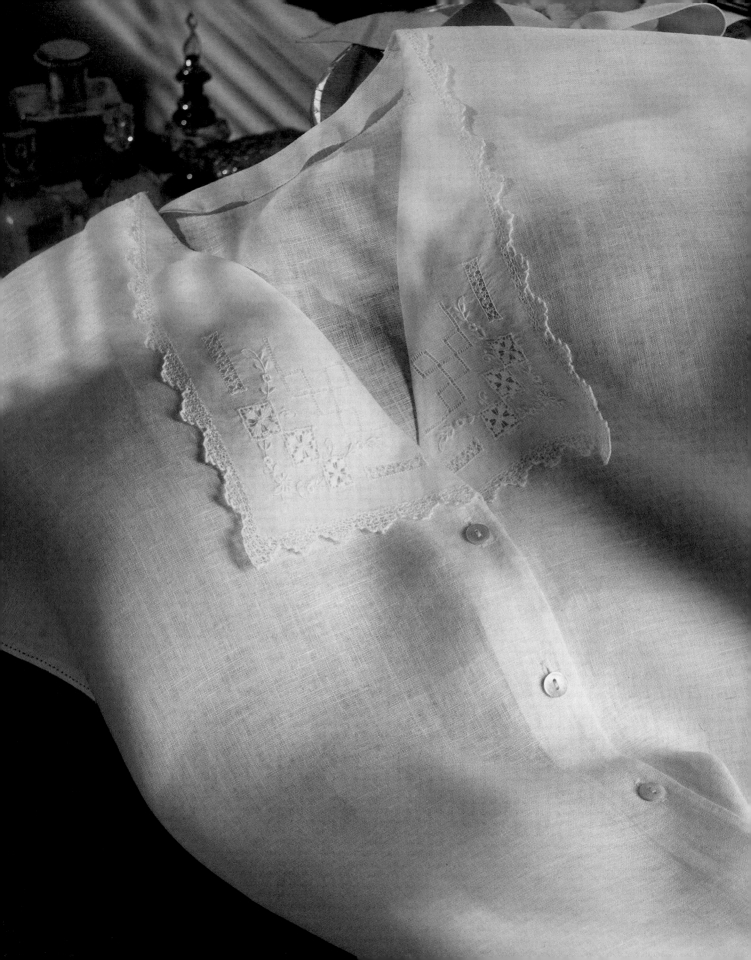

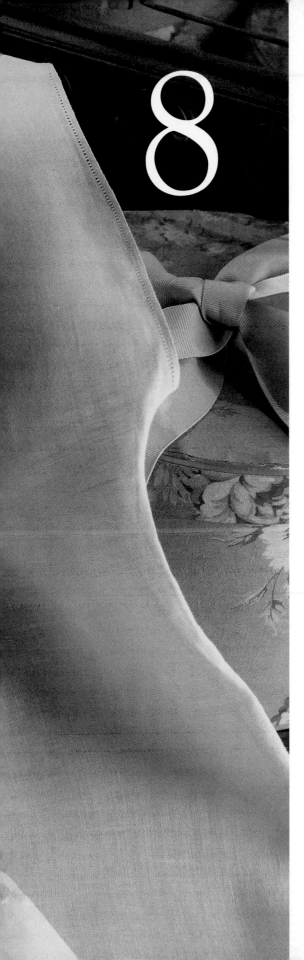

8 Narrow Hemming

A simply beautiful finish to this elegant blouse, the Parisian hemstitch narrow-hems and hemstitches the edges of the cap sleeves in one step. This easy-to-make blouse begins with a V-neck pattern and uses the corners of a handkerchief for the collar.

Narrow hems are called for in many applications. For example, the lower edge of blouses, nightgowns, sheer fabric skirts, circular skirts, and skirt or dress linings are best finished with a narrow hem, as are the edges of ruffles, fabric ties (for aprons or dresses), and tablecloths.

Yet the perfectly stitched narrow hem can be elusive. Pattern instructions for narrow hems usually read something like "Turn edge under ¼ in., press, stitch near fold, trim to ⅛ in., then turn under, press, and stitch again." After many time-consuming efforts following this method resulted only in burned fingertips and uneven, unprofessional-looking hems, I decided to try the narrow hemmers available for my sewing machine. Like many sewers, I was frustrated and disappointed with my first attempts at using these accessories—until I was asked to hem the sides of floor-to-ceiling fabric panels in every pastel color for one of my daughter Emily's dance performances. (This was before home sergers.) After narrow hemming more than 150 yards of broadcloth I knew exactly how to use narrow hemmers! Since then I have taught more than 4,000 people how to narrow hem successfully by sharing a few critical tips that are rarely included in instructions. A little practice definitely helps, but I promise you won't need to hem 150 yards to be able to use your hemmers for quick and neat narrow hems!

Fabric: Mostly light- to medium-weight wovens, although some knits such as tricot can be narrow hemmed (usually with a zigzag-type stitch for a shell edge).

Thread: Appropriate for the fabric; most often Coats Dual Duty Plus extra-fine cotton-covered polyester or fine machine-embroidery cotton threads (size 50/2 or 60/2).

Needle: Appropriate for fabric and thread being used, most often 70 or 80 Universal.

Foot: Narrow hemmer. Choose hemmer according to the fabric weight, the size hem desired, and the stitch to be used. Available hemmers vary by machine (see the photos on the facing page). Typical hemmers include:
• Rolled hemmer. For very lightweight fabrics only. It is used with a zigzag stitch to make a rounded rolled hem, as seen on some handkerchief edges. Some rolled hemmers can also be used with a straight stitch for a tiny flat hem.
• 2mm hemmer. For very lightweight fabrics (e.g., batiste). Makes hems approximately ¹⁄₁₆ in. to ⅛ in. wide.
• 3mm to 4mm hemmers. For light- to medium-weight fabrics (e.g., broadcloth). Makes hems approximately ⅛ in. to ³⁄₁₆ in. wide.
• 5mm to 6mm hemmers. For light- to medium/heavy-weight fabrics (e.g., poplin). Makes hems approximately ¼ in. wide.
• Shell hemmer. Designed to be used with a zigzag-type stitch on lightweight fabrics to create a wider, shell (scallop-like) hem. Depending on the needle-position capability of the machine, sometimes a shell hemmer will also work with a straight stitch.

The size hem that a hemmer will make can be estimated by the size of the curl on the foot, and more accurately by the width of the channel cut out on the underside. Narrow hemming over seams requires a slightly wider hemmer than would otherwise be needed to hem a single layer of the same fabric. For curves, use the narrowest hemmer appropriate for the weight of the fabric.

Some hemmers are designed for straight stitching only; these hemmers have a hole rather than an oval opening for the needle. Some hemmers are designed for the hem to align with a zigzag stitch only; these may be called rolled or shell hemmers. And finally, some more versatile hemmers are designed to be used with either a straight or zigzag-type stitch. Hemmers in the latter two categories both have oval openings for the needle; they cannot usually be distinguished from each other visually.

Difficulties with narrow hemming are often the result of using the wrong foot. Contributing to this problem is the lack of uniform terminology in the sewing industry. The terms "narrow hemmer," "rolled hemmer," and sometimes "shell hemmer" are frequently used interchangeably. It is not uncommon for students in my classes who wanted to straight-stitch narrow hems to have unknowingly purchased a shell hemmer designed to be used with a zigzag stitch. With this type of hemmer a centered straight stitch is too far onto the hem to be secure, and, on some machines, if you move the needle to the next position left, the needle totally misses the hem. When purchasing hemmers, consult a chart from the sewing-machine company or the machine manual to be sure you are getting the foot you need.

A 2mm hemmer comes with some machines. If you do not have a narrow hemmer, a 3mm or 4mm hemmer (usable with either straight or zigzag stitching, if available) is a good middle-range size to purchase.

Stitch: Straight (other stitches for decorative edges will be covered later).

Length: 2mm to 2.5mm or appropriate for fabric.

Upper tension: Normal for fabric used.

Stabilizer: A small piece of light-weight tearaway stabilizer (2 in. to 3 in. square) is helpful when starting the narrow hem at a corner and to hem seams.

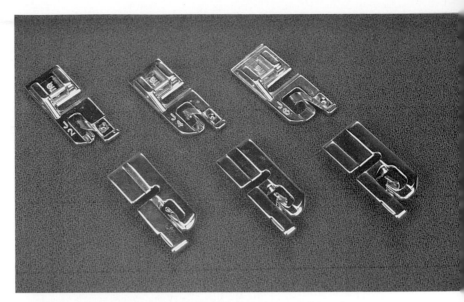

Typical narrow hemmers include (left to right) 2mm, 4mm, and 6mm hemmers. Each makes hems approximately the size of the channel cut out on its underside.

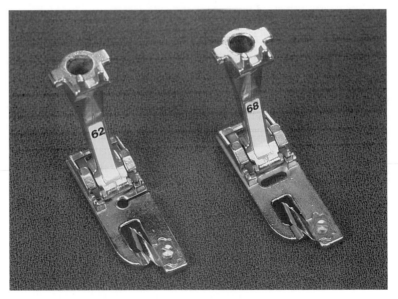

The hemmer at left is designed for straight stitches only (note the small round needle opening); the one at right is a shell hemmer, designed to align with zigzag stitches.

If you are a novice, practice narrow crossgrain (i.e., selvage-to-selvage) hemming with a straight stitch on scraps of batiste using a 2mm hemmer or on broadcloth with a 3mm or 4mm hemmer. Start narrow hemming on a long side about ½ in. or more from a corner. (You can tackle starting at a corner later.) At this stage just get comfortable with guiding the fabric into the hemmer. If you make a mistake, just start again in a new place. There is no need to rip out stitches on these practice pieces.

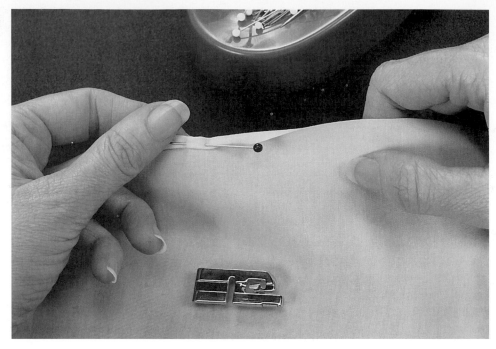

With the fabric wrong side up, form a tiny starting hem by folding the edge over twice and pinning. Make this hem about as wide as the channel on the underside of the foot.

General procedure for narrow hemming

Most narrow hemming is done with a straight stitch, but the instructions that follow also apply to narrow hemming with other stitches. With a little "know-how," you can easily narrow-hem even seemingly difficult areas such as seams and corners.

GETTING STARTED

There are several methods for getting the hem started. This method is easy and works well even on difficult areas, such as starting the hem on a folded double layer of fabric for a shirt and facing.

1. Trim the ravels for a clean edge. (A rotary cutter and mat are great for this task.)

2. With the wrong side of the fabric facing up, form a tiny starting hem by folding the fabric edge over twice where the narrow hem is to begin, as shown in the photo above. Pin with one pin. This hem must be approximately the same width as the channel on the underside of the narrow hemmer.

3. Put the pinned narrow hem under the hemmer foot on the machine and lower the presser foot.

4. Take two to three stitches near the inside folded hem edge (just left of the pin) by turning the flywheel toward you by hand. Stop with the needle down, lift the presser foot (see the photo at top left on the facing page), and remove the pin.

5. Feed the fabric edge into the curl of the hemmer (see the photo at top right on the facing page). You may have to give the fabric in front of the foot a slight tug.

6. Lower the presser foot and slowly begin to stitch. It may be helpful to pull the thread tails gently toward the back for the first few stitches.

After taking two to three stitches, stop with the needle down and lift the presser foot.

After removing the pin, feed the fabric edge into the hemmer curl.

GUIDING THE FABRIC

Perfect narrow hemming requires slight guiding adjustments as you stitch. Using both hands to guide the fabric into the hemmer gives far greater guiding control than using just one hand (see the photo at right).

With the right hand, slightly lift the fabric edge and guide it directly in front of the foot. Allow the fabric to slide freely through your hand. Watch to make sure that the fabric touches the inside of the curl on the right. It should never go under the right toe of the foot.

With the index and middle fingers of the left hand, gently push or pull the fabric at the left front of the foot to adjust how much fabric goes into the foot. Watch to make sure that the fabric edge is at the upper left side of the ditch as it enters the foot. If it is at the center of the foot, there will not be enough fabric for the hem. If it is over the ditch on the left, there will be too much fabric

Two hands are needed for perfect guiding. The right hand guides the fabric edge directly in front of the foot. The index and middle fingers of the left hand gently push (or pull) the fabric at the left front of the foot to keep the fabric edge at the upper left side of the ditch as it enters the foot.

Common feeding mistakes to avoid

With narrow hemming, guiding is critical to success. The photos below show four common feeding mistakes. Slight guiding adjustments will correct these problems.

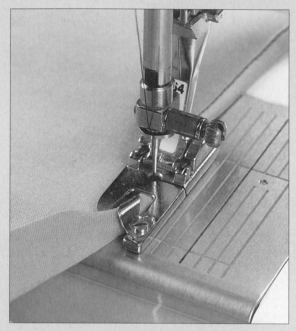

Gap between the fabric and the inside of the curl on the right.

Fabric under the right toe of the foot.

Not enough fabric being fed for the hem.

Too much fabric being fed.

for the hem. The photos on the facing page illustrate some common feeding mistakes to avoid.

Problem solving If the fabric edge is being folded over only once and the raw edge shows, start again and as you stitch, push a little more fabric into the hemmer with the fingers of your left hand. If this happens on a garment, remove the stitches back to the place where the hem is stitched correctly and start again there. No pinning is necessary this time.

If the stitching is in the middle of the hem rather than near the inside folded edge, where it should be, or if extra fabric protrudes from inside the hem, use the fingers of your left hand to feed less fabric into the hemmer.

If the hem is uneven, make sure you keep the fabric edge at the upper left side of the ditch as it enters the foot. Evenness will come with practice.

STARTING AT A CORNER

Some narrow-hemming applications, such as on folded facings or on rectangular scarves, napkins, placemats, and tablecloths, require starting at a corner. Putting stabilizer underneath ensures smooth feeding from the start.

1. Form the starting hem by folding the edge twice at the very beginning of the side to be hemmed. Put about ½ in. of the corner of a small piece of tearaway stabilizer under this starting hem and pin with one pin, as shown in the photo above right.

2. Put the pinned narrow hem under the hemmer foot, lower the presser foot, and take two to three stitches on the pinned hem starting at the edge of the fabric. Stop with the needle down.

3. Lift the presser foot, remove the pin, feed the fabric edge into the curl of the hemmer, and lower the presser foot.

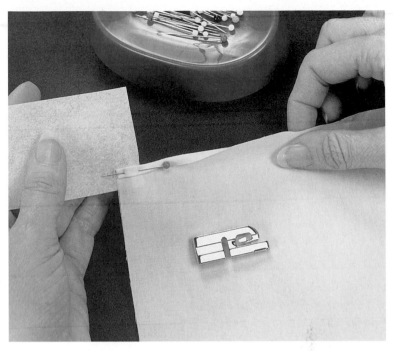

To start narrow hemming at a fabric corner, pin the starting hem to the corner of a piece of tear-away stabilizer.

4. Gently pull the thread tails toward the back as you begin to stitch (see the bottom photo on p. 33). The stabilizer enables the feed dogs to move the fabric easily past the edge without hangups or pushing the fabric down toward the bobbin.

5. Gently tear away the stabilizer when the stitching is complete.

NARROW HEMMING OVER SEAMS

Many applications require narrow hemming over seams. For example, when narrow hemming the lower edge of a blouse, it's necessary to hem over the side seams. By reducing as much bulk as possible, even serged or French seams can be narrow hemmed. (French seams should be made very small if they will be hemmed over.)

1. Secure the seams at the end where the narrow hem will be. Instead of backstitching, which puckers light-

Before narrow hemming over seams, the corners of the lower edge of the seam allowances should be trimmed to reduce bulk; the lower 1 in. of the seam allowances should be held in place with glue stick (or zigzag basting).

Problem solving If the fabric works out of the curl of the foot as the seam goes through, use your left index finger to press on the fabric next to the left side of the foot so the fabric cannot be pushed out.

If the seam gets hung up under the foot, lift the presser foot, put a small piece of tearaway stabilizer under the fabric behind the needle, lower the presser foot, and continue.

ENDING A NARROW HEM

To avoid having a fabric tail protrude at the end of a narrow hem, trim about ¼ in. of the corner before you hem it. (Special situations, such as ending on folded facings and continuous narrow hemming are discussed on the next two pages.)

To keep the fabric in the curl all the way to the end, use your left index finger to press on the fabric next to the left side of the foot, as shown in the photo below.

weight fabric, an easy alternative is to use a very short stitch length (about 1mm) for the lower ½ in. of the seam. Another option is to tie the threads tails together at the end of the seam.

2. To reduce bulk, trim the corners of the lower edge of the seam allowances.

3. Press each seam open or in the desired direction.

4. To keep the seam allowance from shifting, either use fabric glue stick (see the photo above) or zigzag baste (width 3, length 2) to hold the lower 1 in. in place as pressed.

5. Use a hemmer at least 3mm to 4mm wide if seams must be crossed. It is difficult to get seams through a 2mm hemmer.

6. Do not start the hem at a seam. As you approach the seam, stitch slowly and hold the fabric taut to help get over the thickness.

7. Remove any basting after stitching is complete.

To keep the fabric in the curl when hemming seams and at the end of the hem, use your left index finger to press on the fabric next to the left side of the foot.

NARROW-HEMMING THE FACINGS

There are several ways to hem the facings you may encounter when narrow hemming, such as those at the lower edge of a blouse front. This method of narrow hemming the facing and garment together is easy and creates a neat hem with little bulk.

1. Trim the lower edge of facings to eliminate bulk. Trim ¼ in. at the facing edge, angling to nothing near the fold, as shown in the top photo at right.

2. Use glue stick to hold the lower 1 in. of the facing in place to prevent shifting.

3. Fold both the garment fabric and the facing together twice to form the starting hem at the fold, and pin to the corner of a piece of tearaway stabilizer, as instructed on p. 133 in "Starting at a corner" and shown in the middle photo at right. Prepare the hem at the other facing the same way, except pin without stabilizer.

4. Use at least a 3mm to 4mm narrow hemmer. Start as instructed for a corner, except stitch the entire doubled layer before feeding any fabric into the curl of the hemmer (see the bottom photo at right).

5. Continue stitching the narrow hem as usual, until you reach the facing at the other end. At that point stop with the needle down, raise the presser foot, and ease the fabric out of the curl of the foot.

6. Pull the fabric in front of and behind the foot taut to form a matching hem under the foot. (Coax the edge under with your finger, a straight pin, or an awl, if necessary.)

7. Lower the presser foot and stitch the remaining hem. (Remove the pin when you get to it.) For neatness, knot the

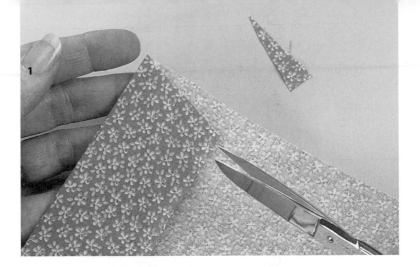

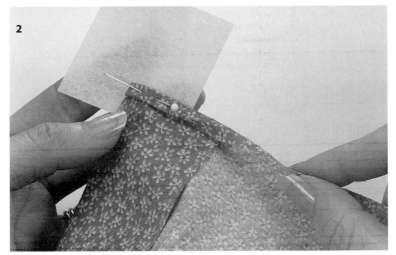

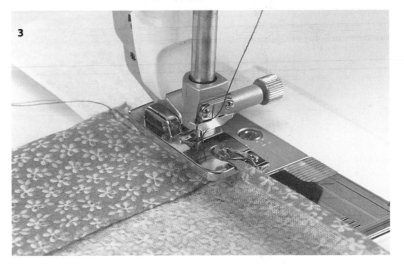

To narrow-hem a garment and facing together (e.g., at a blouse's bottom edge):
1. Trim the lower edge of the facings at an angle to eliminate bulk.
2. Fold both layers of fabric (garment and facing) together twice to form the starting hem, and pin to a piece of tearaway stabilizer.
3. Stitch the entire doubled layer before feeding any fabric into the curl of the hemmer.

thread tails at the end of the stitching, bury about ½ in. of the tails, and trim off the rest.

NARROW-HEMMING CURVES

Gradual curves, such as you would have on round or oval tablecloths and flared skirts, are not difficult to narrow hem. If the curve is tight, reshape it to be more gradual whenever possible. For example, sharp curves on shirt tails can usually be rounded. Use as narrow a hemmer as possible for the weight of the fabric.

Keeping the right amount of fabric fed into the hemmer takes a little more effort on curves. Stitch at a slow speed, and keep the edge of the fabric at the upper left side of the ditch as it enters the foot.

CONTINUOUS NARROW HEMMING

With some applications, such as on flared skirts, round tablecloths, and some blouses, the beginning and end of the narrow hem meet. To join the end of narrow-hem stitching to the place it was started:

1. Stop with the needle down just before the front of the foot reaches the spot the narrow hem began.
2. Lift the presser foot and slide the fabric out of the curl of the foot.
3. Form a matching folded hem on the fabric beneath the foot by pulling the hem slightly taut from in front of and behind the foot. (You may have to use your fingers, a straight pin, or an awl to help form the hem.)
4. Lower the foot and stitch over the folded hem. (The fabric is under the foot, not in the curl for this inch or so of stitching.)
5. Continue until you overlap the beginning of the hem by a few stitches.

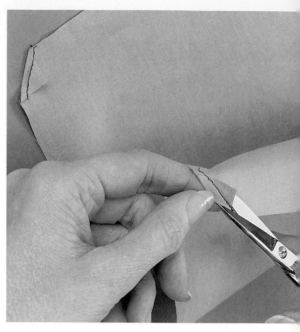

To narrow-hem adjoining sides, first fold the corner to the wrong side and straight stitch across the fold. Trim the excess fabric up to the stitching.

HEMMING ADJOINING SIDES OF A CORNER

This easy method of narrow-hemming adjoining sides, adapted from an Elna educational leaflet, makes an attractive mitered corner with little bulk.

1. Fold about ¼ in. to ⅜ in. of the corner to the wrong side and straight stitch across the fold.
2. Trim the excess fabric up to the stitching, as shown in the photo above.
3. Form the starting hem at the beginning of one side and pin it to the corner of a small piece of tearaway stabilizer, as usual.
4. Continue as instructed on p. 133 for "Starting at a corner," hemming the entire side.
5. Form and pin the starting hem for the adjoining side to stabilizer. Hem this side (see the top photo on the facing page).

After stitching the entire first side, form and pin the starting hem for the next side to stabilizer and continue.

6. After the stitching is complete, gently remove the stabilizer.

7. For a neat appearance, tie and bury the thread tails.

Narrow hemming with specialty stitches

You can use stitches other than straight stitches for narrow hemming to create beautifully finished edges on nightgowns, slips, ruffles (including smocked ruffles), and tablecloths. On some machines you can use utility and decorative stitches with certain narrow hemmers and the stitches will align properly. On other machines two steps are required, in which case the narrow hem is first basted with a straight stitch, then the decorative stitch is sewn over the hem. Either method gives you the option of creating a decorative finish rather than a plain one. The photo above right shows an example.

Narrow hemming combined with the Parisian hemstitch produces a finished decorative edge (sample at upper left) similar to that on a hand-hemstitched handkerchief (sample at lower right).

ONE-STEP METHOD

If the stitch you wish to use aligns as needed on the hem, you can stitch the narrow hem and create the decorative edge at the same time (see the top photo on p. 138). If the stitch does not at first align properly, try the following remedies:

• Check that the stitch is being made in the appropriate direction, and if

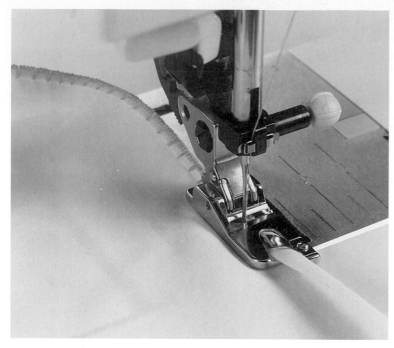

When a decorative stitch aligns properly on the hem, you can narrow-hem and create the decorative edge at the same time (one-step method).

If necessary you can baste the narrow hem first, then add the decorative stitch (two-step method). The narrow hem may be to the right, as shown, or to the left, if necessary, for proper stitch alignment.

necessary, mirror the stitch. If the stitch cannot be mirrored on your machine, look for another similar stitch that is stitched the right direction and try it.
• Try a different stitch width.
• Try a different hemmer.
• If it is possible on your machine to change the needle position with the stitch you are using, try that.
• On some programmable machines, you can program the stitch into memory with the correct alignment.

TWO-STEP METHOD

If the stitch you wish to use cannot be made to align properly, use the two-step method.

1. Baste the narrow hem, using a narrow (usually 3mm or less) hemmer with a long (about 4mm) straight stitch. Upper tension should be loosened.

2. Stitch the utility or decorative stitch over the basted narrow hem to create the desired decorative edge (see the bottom photo at left). If necessary for proper stitch alignment, the fabric may be turned so the narrow hem is to the left. Use a satin-stitch foot and adjust upper tension as needed.

3. Remove the basting stitches.

Finished decorative edges

Shell, picot, scalloped, or hemstitched edges make lovely finishes for delicate garments and table linens. For all the following decorative edges:

  Foot: For the one-step method, use a 2mm to 4mm narrow hemmer with a wide needle hole opening to allow for zigzag stitching. For some machines, these may be called rolled or shell hemmers.

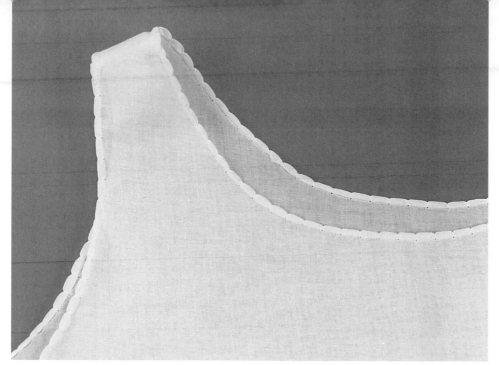

A shell edge creates a soft folded edge that is good for lingerie and baby garments.

T I P

In addition to shell edges, the blind stitch can be used to create decorative shell tucks (see p. 124). Shell tucks are appropriate for the same types of baby, little-girl, and lingerie items as recommended for the shell edging and would be very attractive on a garment on which the neck, armhole, and lower edges were finished with the shell edging.

For the two-step method, use a 2mm or 3mm straight stitch or straight/zigzag stitch narrow hemmer first. Then use a satin-stitch foot for the decorative stitching.

SHELL EDGE

A shell edge is a pretty and practical way to finish edges on baby garments and lingerie (see the photo above). Since it creates a very soft folded edge, it is especially useful for finishing neck and armhole edges on slips and gowns where lace or other finishings may be too rough for these sensitive skin areas.

Fabric: Soft, lightweight woven fabric such as batiste. Tricot may also be used.

Thread: Fine cotton (size 50/2 or 60/2) or extra-fine cotton-wrapped polyester.

Needle: Appropriate for fabric and thread, most often 70 Universal.

Stitch: Blind stitch (also called blind hem stitch) or a variation of it. This stitch creates an edging that more

closely resembles a handsewn shell edge than a simple zigzag stitch will. Mirror-imaging may be necessary for the zigzag part of the stitch to go to the right as illustrated.

Width: Varies with hemmer. Start with 3.5mm to 4.5mm, then adjust.

Length: Varies with machine. Start with about 1.5mm, then adjust. Each shell or scallop should be no longer than ³⁄₈ in.

Upper tension: Slightly tightened (adjusted to a higher number) so that there is enough pull to form the shell shape.

1. Start the narrow hem as usual, except stitch until there is a zigzag stitch to hold the starting hem before you feed the fabric into the curl of the hemmer. 2. For proper alignment, the straight stitches in the stitch pattern should go into the single layer of fabric just to the left of the hem. The zigzag must go "into the air" just to the right of the hem. If the alignment is wrong, try the

Blind stitch

Variation of blind stitch

suggestions listed for the one-step method on pp. 137-138. If none helps, use the two-step method instead (see p. 138), and baste the narrow hem with a long straight stitch first. Then stitch over it with a blind stitch to create the shell effect. Remove the basting.

Problem solving If the shell effect is not being formed, tighten upper tension. If there is puckering, loosen (decrease) upper tension.

For curves, use the narrowest hemmer that will give the desired results. If the curve is very sharp and cannot be reshaped, consider using a different edge finish.

PICOT OR SCALLOPED EDGES

Stretch blind stitch

The stretch blind stitch and the edging scallop—the same stitches used for the decorative edges described in Chapter 3—can be combined with narrow hemming for a more finished edge.

Edging scallop

Fabric: Medium-weight wovens (broadcloth, most cotton or polycotton prints) with the stretch blind stitch for the picot decorative edge; lightweight wovens (batiste) for the edging scallop.

Thread: Fine machine-embroidery thread—size 50/2 or 60/2 cotton or size 40 rayon.

Needle: 80 Universal on broadcloth, 70 Universal on batiste.

Stitch: Stretch blind stitch; edging scallop. Engage mirror imaging if necessary to make the stitches in the direction shown.

A simple zigzag can also be used with some hemmers for a finished decorative edge; the narrow hem will roll rather than stay flat. A relatively close zigzag (width 2.5mm to 3mm, length 1mm) with a 2mm or rolled hemmer makes an especially attractive decorative edge for ruffles.

Width: Start at about 4mm, then adjust.

Length: Start at about .5mm, then adjust.

Upper tension: Slightly loosened for picot; slightly tightened for scallop. Test.

Problem solving The right side of the stitch must clear the folded hem edge on the right. If the alignment is wrong, try the remedies suggested for the one-step method (see p. 137-138). If none of these helps, use the two-step method (see p. 138). Baste the narrow hem with a long straight stitch. Then stitch over it with either the stretch blind stitch or the edging scallop. Remove the basting.

HEMSTITCHED HANDKERCHIEF EDGE

If your machine has the Parisian hemstitch (also called pin stitch or point de Paris) or the picot stitch, you can combine either stitch with narrow hemming for a beautiful hemstitched edge, as shown in the bottom photo on p. 137 and on the armhole edges of the blouse in the photo on pp. 126-127.

Fabric: Appropriate for hemstitching; mostly linen and cotton.

Thread: Very fine machine-embroidery cotton (80/2, 70/2, or 60/2).

Needle: Most often 120 Universal. Experiment with others.

Stitch: Parisian hemstitch (pin stitch, point de Paris) or picot. Engage mirror imaging if necessary to form the stitch in the direction shown.

Width: Varies. Start at about 2mm, then adjust.

Length: Varies. Start at about 2.5mm, then adjust.

Upper tension: Normal to slightly tightened to create enlarged holes.

Problem solving For this edge, the forward and reverse stitches must be on the single layer of fabric to the left of the narrow hem, and the zigzag part of the stitch should go to the right to catch the hem. If you are unable to get this alignment with either of these stitches, use the two-step method (see p. 138). Use a regular needle (70 or 80 Universal) to baste the narrow hem with a long straight stitch. Then switch to the larger needle to hemstitch over it.

to the wrong side as usual, except use a long straight stitch, then turn the fabric over and stitch the decorative stitch from the right side. As always, test your setup on a scrap first.

Picot or scalloped edges can be created by stitching over a folded edge and trimming from the back (see pp. 46-49), or by combining the stitches with narrow hemming for a more finished edge. When would you choose one method over the other?

On projects where durability is important, the narrow-hemmed decorative edge is probably a better choice. Depending on the fabric however, a narrow-hemmed edge may be too bulky and stiff for some projects, like gathered ruffles for example. Of course, personal preference is a consideration also. One method may be easier to do or may look better on a certain fabric or location on a garment than the other method.

Parisian hemstitch

Picot stitch

Questions

When narrow hemming with a decorative stitch to create a picot, scalloped, or hemstitched edge, which side of the fabric do you use as the right side?

With solid-color fabrics without seams (for example, tablecloths, or ruffles before they are attached), you can use whichever side you like best as the right side.

On projects with seams, you probably want the narrow hem to turn to the wrong side. Stitch a test sample on the fabric. If the underside of the stitch (on the right side of the fabric) doesn't look just as nice as the top side (often it does), adjusting upper tension should help. An alternative is to use the two-step method (see p. 138). Narrow-hem

What to Look for in a Sewing Machine

The goal of this book is to help you use the sewing machine you have to its fullest potential. But because I am constantly asked for machine recommendations, I have included in this appendix a discussion of the features that I look for in a sewing machine for fine machine sewing. The information can be helpful for understanding features you have on your current machine, as well as for when you are in the market for a new machine.

Not everyone wants or needs the same capabilities on a sewing machine. Like many home sewers, I do general garment construction, mending and hemming, and home decorating. If handling these applications was all I wanted from a machine, many basic machines would serve my needs. Even for most machine heirloom sewing techniques, such as attaching laces and entredeux, a good straight and zigzag machine (one that has good-quality tension and feeding for handling the lightweight fabrics) is all that is required. However, once I became fascinated with machine versions of related fine machine sewing techniques like hemstitching, fagoting, and shadow work, my machine wants became more sophisticated. As shown throughout this book, many of these techniques are possible on mechanical machines; but the capabilities and features that have developed with the computerized sewing machines have opened up creative possibilities we never would have dreamed possible just a few years ago.

Stitches

Accommodating the display and selection of large numbers of stitches has become a major challenge for machine companies. In addition to checking the availability of certain stitches on a particular machine, it is important to consider the user friendliness of the stitch display and selection process. Along with good basic utility stitches (straight, zigzag, blind hem, multiple zigzag for mending and sewing elastic, double overlock for some seaming, and consistent good-quality buttonholes), I look for the following:

Of the hemstitches, I look principally for the **Parisian** stitch to resemble pin stitching by hand and the **Venetian** stitch to resemble entredeux. Other stitches that are not used as much as the Parisian and Venetian, but are nice to have for decorative rows, include the **four-sided, triple honeycomb** or **Rhodes,** and **Turkish** stitches. The last two stitches resemble the honeycomb and the double overlock stitches, but each step of the stitch pattern is repeated, which is necessary for hemstitching.

For related techniques I look for the **feather** or **briar** stitch for decorative embroidery and fagoting, the **tracery scallop** for twin-needle shadow-work scallops and the **edging scallop,** which creates scallops over a folded edge without necessitating trimming around each scallop. I also look for other scallops that make pretty decorative stitches, even though trimming is necessary when they are used for edging.

Finally I look for any other decorative stitches (such as flowers, leaves, bows, and so forth) that would be appropriate for creating the look of hand embroidery or purchased Swiss embroideries.

General features

Most upper-end machines have a majority of the following features, but take note whether the ones you care about most are easy to identify (have readily identifiable symbols) and are convenient for you to select and use.

Good-quality, well-marked tension mechanisms While the newer "automatic, self-adjusting" tension systems are great, the upper tension setting nonetheless should be adjusted to obtain the best results for certain fabrics or techniques. The dial should be well marked, so that you can easily note the adjusted setting for future reference, before returning to the normal setting.

Good-quality feeding mechanism Good feeding and tension are both crucial for any sewing, but especially for sewing on lightweight fabrics and for techniques like fagoting. The feeding mechanism must hold the fabric firmly and move it evenly.

The following features are helpful, but not absolutely necessary.

Ability to stop with needle up/down as desired Engaging "needle down" allows you to adjust fabric as you go without shifting the fabric under the foot. It is also helpful when pivoting the fabric to turn a corner, especially with decorative stitches. Since I use this feature often, I like to be able to engage it with a button right over the needle bar or with the foot pedal.

Ability to stop automatically at the end of the stitch pattern This function is also very helpful for turning corners with hemstitches and other decorative stitches, for example, when stitching around a square collar.

Speed reducer An even, slow to medium sewing speed gives the best results for decorative stitching. Stitching at all-out speed or at a very uneven speed (pumping) can affect tension, stitch length, and the general quality of the decorative stitch.

For decorative sewing, including twin-needle stitching, I usually engage the speed reducer, which allows me to stitch up to a medium speed, but gives me much more control for a smooth sewing rhythm.

Stitch width and length features
The indicators should be easy to read, visible at all times, and well marked (ideally with meaningful numbers, i.e., millimeters). Settings should be easy to change (i.e., not requiring multiple steps) and changeable in small increments—automatic settings are often too wide and too long, so the ability to override them and make adjustments in small increments is desirable.

A wide stitch width (6mm or wider), though not often needed, is useful for fagoting and for a prettier shape for scallops (especially twin-needle scallops) as well as for other decorative stitches.

Balancing or fine adjustment/tuning mechanism The mechanism to balance stitch alignment should be easy to use, and the adjustments should be indicated with numbers or with a position that is easy to record accurately for future reference (see the sidebar on p. 74).

Ability to change needle positions with as many stitches as possible
Being able to change needle positions ensures that the desired stitch can be aligned as necessary for the desired foot. For example, it is possible to combine decorative stitches, such as the edging scallop or Parisian hemstitch, with narrow hemming, but changing needle positions is often necessary for proper alignment.

Ability to use twin-needles Twin needles are needed for twin-needle pintucks and twin-needle shadow work.

Mirror imaging with as many stitches as possible The ability to mirror the stitch (ideally, horizontally as well as vertically) often comes in handy. For example, mirroring enables you to stitch the project in the most convenient position—with the bulk of the garment to the left and out of the way—for hemming or for sewing both sides of a trim or lace with decorative stitches, such as the Parisian hemstitch. Mirroring is also useful for combining decorative patterns (for example, leaf and flower patterns) in the most attractive way.

Convenient reverse button An instant reverse button in a convenient location, such as right over the needle bar, is very handy. You don't want to have to take your eyes off your work to find the button.

Embroidery and programming capabilities It is now possible to create your own embroidery design combinations, including ones that can look very much like expensive Swiss embroideries. If this type of work interests you, check whether the embroidery designs are appropriate for the uses you intend and check the size of the designs—many machines now allow designs to be elongated while maintaining the same density. (This feature makes a broader size range possible with the desired density for satin stitches such as scallops.) Also consider the ease or difficulty of programming and editing.

Special features

Table For a freearm machine a large, removable sewing surface allows for more control when guiding.

Thread cutter/holder It should be in a convenient location to cut threads after stitching and hold them for the beginning of the next stitching.

Needle threader It should be easy to use and preferably built in.

Securing or tie-off option This is very useful for securing the beginning and end of embroidery motifs.

Light Brightness and location are both important.

Low-bobbin warning It should be readily visible.

Portability Nothing beats classes for "hands-on" learning of all the wonderful things you can do on your machine. But classes mean you will regularly have to transport your machine (for more on this subject, see p. 146). Check how easy the machine is to pack up and how heavy it is to carry.

Updateability Since the marriage of computer technology and home sewing machines, machines are changing much more rapidly than in the past. Some machine companies make additional stitches available, usually in the form of cassettes. If you are interested in decorative stitching, this is an advantage, since you do not have to purchase a new machine to get more stitches. However, it is important to realize that a machine company will not keep making cassettes or accessories for previous models indefinitely.

The top-of-the-line Pfaffs since the 1471 have allowed the home sewer, with increasing technological refinement, to input each step of a stitch pattern into the machine. Other machine companies are now adding some capability to create stitch designs. Even though most home sewers do not regularly use this function, it is nice to know you can add stitches.

Good instruction manual   Since most machines are imported, the manuals are often awkwardly translated from a foreign language. Check the clarity of the instructions, and of the photos or illustrations. A good index in the back of the book and a table of contents in front make looking up specific information easier. It is very helpful to have all the presser feet and stitches named and illustrated with suggested uses. (Many machine companies have additional instructional materials available—a workbook, leaflets, magazines, and so on.)

Brand-specific features   There are a few other advantageous features that are unique to certain machines (at least for now). For example, some Berninas have a knee lift and the ability to return to the last settings you used with a stitch; some Elnas have bobbin-tension bypass for easily sewing right side down with heavier threads on the bobbin; some Pfaffs have built-in dual feed; and several machines, including some New Homes and Vikings, now have outstanding large embroidery motif capabilities. No one machine has absolutely everything!

Presser feet and accessories

I probably would not reject a machine that I loved just because of deficiencies in the presser feet. Although they are not usually ideal, feet from different machines are sometimes interchangeable. (Test before relying on being able to interchange feet, however.) Refer to pp. 13-18 for more detail.

Identification   Feet and accessories should have identification on them so that you can tell easily what you have and can track down its intended purpose in the manual or from a dealer if necessary.

Instructions   If good instructions on using an accessory are not in the machine manual, they should be included with the purchase of the accessory.

Availability of special feet   The standard zigzag, satin-stitch (embroidery), buttonhole, zipper, and blind-hem feet should come with the machine. (Ideally they should easily snap on and off a shank on the needle bar and be stored in a compartment conveniently located on the machine.) Find out whether the additional presser feet you want most are available for the machine.

Price   Additional feet should be reasonably priced; if they are too costly, you may be reluctant to purchase them.

Ease of use   Test-sew with the presser feet you expect to use the most. Certain special feet available for some machines, particularly narrow hemmers and pintuck feet, yield good results very easily, while using those for other machines seems like a battle.

Choosing a dealer

When you are in the market for a new machine, make a list of the features you want most. There will likely be several machines that will fit your needs. When you have decided which ones to consider, make an appointment before going to test them to be sure the dealer will be available.

Take pieces of the fabrics you use most. (Many dealers will have only starched, stiff "demo" cloth available.) Ask to stitch the techniques you are most interested in (including buttonholes) yourself. Remember, for the best results the thread and needles

should be changed to those appropriate for each fabric and technique.

The helpfulness of the dealer is definitely a consideration. A dealer's knowledge about the particular kind(s) of sewing you do, while not absolutely necessary, is an asset, because it will mean more reliable tips, recommendations for the best feet and accessories, and help with troubleshooting when you have stitching problems.

Classes provided by the dealer are very important. Inquire about which ones are included with machine purchase. Also check on the warranty and how the dealer handles service.

Price is usually a big concern, of course. Ask the dealer to let you know when the model you like goes on sale. Also, you may want to consider a used machine. Often perfectly good used machines are available because their owners just wanted to upgrade.

All this will take time. Do not let yourself be pressured into a hurried decision. A sewing machine is a major purchase, and you will be happier if you have taken the time to find the best machine and dealer combination for you.

Upgrading

I would recommend upgrading when your present machine no longer meets your sewing needs. If all you want to do is basic sewing and you have a machine that does a good job of it, then buying a new, top-of the-line machine does not make sense. But if you wish you could finish edges with a pretty decorative scallop (that you don't have to trim around) or attach lace with the Parisian hemstitch, for example, then it is worth taking the time to investigate machines that satisfy your wish list. The other time to consider upgrading is whenever your current machine needs repairs that cost more than you want to spend.

Caring for Your Sewing Machine

It is well worth the little time and effort it takes to care properly for your sewing machine, both for maintaining the stitching quality and for avoiding the inconvenience and cost of repairs.

Cleaning and oiling

Before starting a sewing project and any time you are having stitching problems, clean your sewing machine. Follow the instructions in your machine manual.

Occasionally (about every three to six months, depending on your sewing habits) do a more thorough cleaning. Clean out any lint, dust, threads, broken needles, sequins, and any other foreign objects. (Children put some amazing things into sewing machines!) Most routine machine cleaning can be done adequately with a brush. But occasionally I use "canned air" to remove lint that cannot be reached with a brush. (Blowing into machines with your mouth is not recommended.) Just be sure to aim the nozzle so that lint is forced out of the machine, not farther into it. There are also many kinds of mini-vacuums and vacuum attachments available.

Use a soft cloth to wipe any visible lint or dust from the outside of the machine. The needle bar in particular collects a lot of greasy fuzz and should be wiped. Remove any sticky residue on spool spindles with rubbing alcohol. If rubbing alcohol will not remove the sticky residue that tape and labels may leave on presser feet, spool spindles, or the machine bed, try Goo Gone or Goof Off, both available at hardware stores. As always, test on an inconspicuous area. Stains on the outside of the machine can usually be cleaned safely with Formula 409 or similar product, but check with your dealer or test first.

"Floss" the tension discs to remove the buildup of residue from some threads, especially poor-quality threads. Raise the presser bar to the up position and set the upper tension dial to "0". Fold a piece of soft (but not fuzzy) cotton fabric in half and put some rubbing alcohol along the fold. Now slide the fold up and down through the tension discs, as if flossing. (If there is a separating plate, floss each side.) Remember to return your tension dial to the normal setting afterwards.

If oiling is recommended for your machine (check the manual), oil it after cleaning. Use only the sewing-machine oil recommended for your machine. After oiling, run the machine unthreaded to work the oil in, then "sew" (without thread) a fabric scrap to absorb any excess oil.

Almost all oilers leak unless kept upright. I keep mine upright in a cup or compartment with other sewing notions near my machine, rather than in the accessory tray.

Some oilers look very much like Fray Check containers, and several sewers I know have damaged their sewing machines by inadvertently "Fray Checking" instead of oiling them. To prevent this, do not store the two containers near each other and consider replacing the oiler with one that looks very different. Machine dealers usually carry inexpensive oil containers.

Maintenance and repair

Some machine companies suggest a schedule for routine dealer maintenance and others don't. Check your machine manual and ask your dealer for recommendations, but use common sense too. There are many variables that affect how often your machine will need professional care, the main factor being how careful you are about keeping your machine clean and oiled (if your machine requires oil). If you keep your machine covered when not in use and clean it often, it will need maintenance far less often than the machine that is not so well cared for. Generally computer machines are more sensitive to lint than older mechanical models and should be serviced more often. Other factors affecting maintenance schedule include how often you sew, the kind of sewing you do, your climate, and of course, stitching quality.

Whenever you take your machine for service, include a few scraps of the types of fabrics you stitch the most so that the machine can be adjusted and tested on those fabrics.

When you are having stitching problems, first run through the troubleshooting routine on p. 6 and check the problem-solving section of your machine manual. When it is necessary to take the machine in for repair, leave it set up as it was when the problem occurred (i.e., same thread, needle, and so on). Also take a sample of the stitched fabric that shows the problem. This will help the dealer find out what's wrong.

Power surges and magnets

Surge protectors give some protection, but cannot prevent damage to a sewing machine from lightning or a severe power surge. If your area is prone to power surges or lightning, it makes good sense to disconnect your machine from the power between uses, or at least during storms. You may disconnect the power cord at the outlet or at the machine. If you disconnect it at the machine and the other end of the cord is still plugged into the outlet, do not leave the cord touching the machine.

145

Representatives from Bernina, Elna, New Home, and Viking/White all say that the magnets in magnetic pincushions are not strong enough to cause problems with their machines. Pfaff representatives recommend that magnetic pincushions not actually touch their machines.

Transporting your machine

To travel with your machine, position it so that it cannot topple. To prevent theft, do not leave it unattended if it is visible. Avoid leaving a machine in a trunk or closed car on very hot days. Cold temperatures should not damage your machine, but may cause it to run sluggishly until the lubrication warms up. You can avoid this problem by let-ting the machine warm to room temperature before you start sewing.

For long-distance transporting, the best protection is to pack a machine in the fitted Styrofoam pieces and box in which it originally came. It is rare for a machine packed this way to be damaged. If you need a box and no longer have yours, a dealer may have extras and be willing to lend or give you one that will work.

For air travel, to a sewing seminar, for example, many sewing educators recommend putting the machine, packed in its box, into a large soft-sided piece of luggage. Fill in any space around the box with fabric, clothes, and so on. The luggage conceals that fact that you have a valuable item (which helps prevent theft), provides a handle for carrying, and makes it less likely that you will have to sign a waiver. The airlines I consulted said they are liable for up to $1250 per passenger for properly packed checked baggage. (Some offer additional coverage for a fee.) You may hand-carry your machine, but then in most cases you are totally responsible for it. Check with your homeowners' insurance company to see if it will cover any damage or theft that the airline will not.

All the machine companies I surveyed (Bernina, Elna, New Home, Pfaff, and Viking/White) said that airport security devices will not harm their machines.

Resources

Sources of Supply

Buttons 'n' Bows   14086 Memorial Drive, Houston, TX 77079; (713) 496-0170

Clotilde*   2 Sew Smart Way, B8031, Stevens Point, WI; 54481-8031; (800) 772-2891

Linen and Lace   6544 Riverside Drive, Dublin, OH 43017; (614) 889-7581

Londa's Sewing Etc.   404 South Duncan Road, Champaign, IL 61821; (217) 352-2378

Margaret Pierce, Inc.*   P.O. Box 4542, Greensboro, NC 27404; (910) 292-6430

Miss Maureen's   1151 Hillcrest Road, Suite E, Mobile, AL 36695; (800) 699-0991

Nancy's Notions*   333 Beichl Avenue, P.O. Box 683, Beaver Dam, WI 53916-0683; (800) 833-0690

The Needle Sharpe   3261 Mendon Road, Cumberland, RI 02864-2415; (401) 658-1106

Peanut Butter-n-Jelly Kids   3607 Old Shell Road, Mobile, AL 36608; (334) 342-8017

The Smocking Horse Collection   5 Parkway Drive, Olmsted Falls, OH 44138; (800) 910-2035

Speed Stitch*   3113 Broadpoint Drive, Harbor Heights, FL 33983; (800) 874-4115

Ardare Cottage   142 Allan Street, Kyabram, Victoria 3620, Australia; (058) 52-2215

* indicates mail order only

Publications

The Creative Machine (a quarterly magazine for machine sewers), P.O. Box 2634, Menlo Park, CA 94026-2634; (415) 366-4440.

Creative Needle (a bimonthly magazine for smocking, heirloom sewing, and related needle-art enthusiasts), 1 Apollo Road, Lookout Mountain, GA 30750; (800) 443-3127.

Sew Beautiful (a bimonthly magazine for heirloom-sewing, smocking, and related needle-art enthusiasts), 518 Madison Street, Huntsville, AL 35801-4286; (205) 533-9568.

Threads (a bimonthly magazine for sewers), 63 S. Main Street, P.O. Box 5506, Newtown, CT 06470-5506; (203) 426-8171.

Machine Settings for Decorative Techniques

This chart provides the stitch numbers for several brands and models of sewing machines. Suggested starting settings for stitch width and length are in parentheses.

The machines included in the chart are those with which I am most familiar—the machines brought to my classes the most. There are many other machines capable of most of these techniques. If your machine is not included in this chart, use the stitch illustrations and descriptions plus the guidelines for settings at the beginning of each technique in the appropriate chapter to determine how to set your machine.

MACHINE	Edging, Appliqué		Twin Needle	Hemstitches		Fagoting
	Picot	Scalloped	Shadow Work**	Parisian	Venetian	
Bernina						
930	5* (W 4, L .5)		20 (W 3, L 1)			6 red (W 4, L 2)
1090	same as 930		19 (W 4, L .75)			13 (W 5, L 1.5)
1130, 1230, & 1260	5* (W 4, L .3)	23 (W 4, L .3)	24 (W 2.5, L .75)	26 (W 2, L 2)	18 (W 3.5, L 1.3, balance -2, long stitch button)	11 (13 on 1130), continuous reverse, (auto), balance +25
1530	A2/5* (W 4, L .3)	H1/7* (W 4, L .3)	H1/8 (W 3, L 1)	H1/4 (W 2, L 2)	H1/5 (W 3, L 2.5)	A1/9, continuous reverse, (auto), balance+25
1630	same as 1530	G1/7* (W 4, L .3)	G1/8 (same as 1530)	G1/4 (W 2, L 2)	G1/5 (W 3, L 2.5)	same as 1530
Elna						
Carina and most disc models	built-in 2 (W 4, L .5)	built-in 3 (W 4, L .5)	disc 4 (W 3.5, L 1)	disc 126 (W 4)	disc 140 (W 4)	disc 104 (W 4)
7000	5 (W 4.4, L .5)	15 (W 5, L .6)	14 (W 3.1, L 1.2)	746 (W 1.8, L 2.5)	747 (W 3.7)	742 or 721 (auto)
8000	6 (same as 7000)	14 (W 5, L .5)	81 (same as 7000)	68 (W 1.8, L 2.5)	69 (W 3.7)	71 or 62 (auto)
9000, Diva	same as 8000	86 (same as 8000)	90 (W 3.7, L 1.2)	120 (W 1.8, L 2.5)	121 (W 3.7)	127 or 891 cassette 2 (W 5, L 1.8)
9006	21 (W 5.5, L .45)	38 (W 5, L .35)	27 (W 4, L 1)	24 (W 2, L 2.5)	70 (program 31 times, size 1-2)	25 (W 5, L 2)
Kenmore						
385-19601	31 (W 3.5, L .3)		22 (W 3, L 1)	30 (W 2.5, L 2)		25 (W 5.5, L 2.5)

* Mirror image or put fold to the left.

** Width will vary with twin needles and presser foot. Test carefully.

Machine Settings for Decorative Techniques

MACHINE	Edging, Appliqué		Twin Needle	Hemstitches		Fagoting
	Picot	Scalloped	Shadow Work**	Parisian	Venetian	
New Home (Janome)						
6000	26 (W 4, L .5)		22 (W 3, L 2)	I 27 (W 2.5, L 2.5)	II 81 (W 4, L 3)	19 (auto)
7000	15 (W 4, L .4)	29 (W 5, L .35)	same as 6000	16 (W 2.5, L 2.5)	53 (W 3, L auto)	17 (W 5, L 2)
7500	43 (W 5.5, L .4)	60 (same as 7000)	47 (W 4, L 1)	44 (W 2.5, L 2.5)	84 (W 3)	45 (same as 7000)
8000	21 (W 5.5, L .45)	38 (same as 7000)	27 (same as 7500)	24 (W 2, L 2.5)	70 (program 31 times, size 1-2)	25 (same as 7000)
9000	150* (W 4, L .3)	52 (same as 7000)	148 (same as 7500)	26 (same as 8000)	81 (50%)	28 (same as 7000)
Pfaff						
1471	18 (W 4.5, L .5)		38 (W 4, L 14)	78 (W 3, L 2.5)	programmable*** (W 3, L 2.5)	29 (W 6, L 2.5)
1473	17 (same as 1471)	54 (W 4.5, L .4, balance 6)	same as 1471	I65 (W 2, L 3)	169 (W 3.5, L 2.5)	same as 1471
1475	same as 1473	same as 1473	same as 1471	same as 1473	same as 1473	same as 1471
7530	5 (same as 1471)	51 (W 5, L 8)	program an arch	97 (W 2, L 2.5)	100 (W 3.5, L 3)	17 (auto)
7550, 7570	5 (same as 1471)	61 (W 4.5, L 8)	141 (W 4, L 9) or program an arch	112 (same as 7530)	115 (W 4, L 2.5)	17 (W 6, L 2.5)
Viking						
6000 series	cam A orange (W 4, L .3)	cam G green (W 4, L .3)	cam D red or H green (W 3, L .3)	cam C yellow		cam D yellow (W 4)
990	built-in 10 (W 4, L .3)		2-8 (W 3, L 1)	2-3 (W 2, L 2.5)		2-19 (W 6, L 2.5)
500	10 (W 4.5, L .3)		32 (W 3.5, L 1.5)	12 (same as 990)	13 (auto)	34 (W 5.5, L 2)
1100, #1, and 1+	A29 (W 4.5, L .2)	D29* (W 4.5, L .5, elongate 1)	A32 (W 3.5, L 2)	D6 (same as 990)	D7 (auto)	A35 (same as 500)

* Mirror image or put fold to the left.

** Width will vary with twin needles and presser foot. Test carefully.

*** Venetian hemstitch program for Pfaff 1471 (Courtesy of Louise Gerigk at Pfaff):
    width   18 02 18 34 18 18 18 18
    length 00 14 28 14 00 28 00 28

Index

A

Appliqué:
  corded, 51
  fabric for, 49
  machine settings for, 147-148
  needles for, 50
  preparation for, 50-51
  shadow, 87-88
  stitches for, 48-49
  thread for, 49
Arcs, stitching, 32

B

Backache, preventing, 39
Balancing, of stitch alignment, 74
Blind stitch:
  for blind hemming, 117
  for shell edge, 139
Bobbins:
  labeling, 10, 11
  storing, 10
  tension adjustment for, 10, 20, 25
  winding, 10, 11
Bracket stitch, for shadow work, 61
Briar stitch, for fagoting, 102
Buttonholes:
  cording, 23
  cutting, 23
  sewing, 22-23

C

Circles, stitching, 32
Coffee stirrer, as fagoting guide,
  32, 103, 104
Cord:
  cutting, 78
  for corded edges, 45
  for corded hemstitching, 76
  for corded twin-needle stitching, 56
Crease lines, concealing, 121-124
Cross stitch:
  for built-in hemstitching, 73
  for fagoting, 102
Cutting, accuracy in, 28

D

Daisy stitch, for built-in hemstitching,
  73

Dental-floss threaders, as sewing aids,
  59, 60, 76
Directional stitching, 40, 65

E

Edges:
  corded, 44-45
    zigzag stitch for, 45
  hemstitched handkerchief edge,
    140-141
  'no-trim-around' scalloped, 44, 47-48
    edging scallop stitch for, 48
    machine settings for, 147-148
    with narrow hemming, 140
  picot, 44, 46-47
    machine settings for, 147-148
    with narrow hemming, 140
    stretch blind stitch for, 46
    stretch stitch for, 46
  picot, corded, 51
  raw, finishes for, 105
  shell, 139-140
    blind stitch for, 139
Edging scallop stitch:
  for finished scalloped edge, 140
  for 'no-trim-around' scalloped edge,
    47-48
Entredeux:
  machine methods for, 96-98, 113
  See also Venetian hemstitch.
Eyestrain, preventing, 39

F

Fabric:
  for appliqué, 48-49
  grain direction in, 7
  for hemstitching, 68
  lightweight, sewing with, 22
  for narrow hems, 128
  oversize, for decorative stitching, 28
  for pintucks, 58
  prewashing, 7, 88
  for shadow work, 61
  for twin-needle stitching, 55-56
Fagoting:
  alternative methods for, 104
  with appliqué cord and Venetian
    hemstitch, 110
  block capital letter "I" stitch for, 102

briar stitch for, 102
  on corded edges, 104
  cross stitch for, 102
  defined, 102
  fabric-to-fabric, 102
    with appliqué cord, 112
  feather stitch for, 102
  herringbone stitch for, 102
  honeycomb stitch for, 102
  lace-to-fabric, 108
    with appliqué cord, 111
  lace-to-lace, 108-109
    with appliqué cord, 111
  laces for, 107-108
  machine settings for, 147-148
  multiple-zigzag stitch for, 102
  problem-solving tips for, 103
  stitches for, 102
  and tension adjustment, 102, 113
  thread for, 102
  uses for, 102
  Venetian hemstitch for, 102
Fagoting plates, as guides, 103
Feather stitch, for fagoting, 102
Feet. See Presser feet.
Fil tiré, on sewing machine, 85-86
Four-sided hemstitch:
  for built-in hemstitching, 73
  over cord or ribbon, 79
  for machine-made fil tiré, 85-86

G

Gathering:
  stitch length for, 18
  technique for, 38
Glue stick, fabric vs. multi-purpose,
  50-51
Grain:
  lengthwise vs. crosswise, and
    puckering, 7
  straightening, 28
Guides:
  coffee stirrers as, 32, 103, 104
  needle plates as, 29, 31
  presser feet as, 30-31
  rubber bands as, 32
  seam, 31
  tape as, 32
  See also Guiding.

Guiding:
for accuracy and comfort, 39
for decorative stitching, 38
discussed, 29
for edgestitching, 38
for fagoting, 32, 103, 104
needle position and, 29-30
for overlock seams, 36
for topstitching, 38
for understitching, 38
See also Guides.

H

Hemming:
blind,
blind stitch for, 117
fabric preparation for, 117-118
'in-the-air' method for, 116,
119-120
presser feet for, 117
standard method for, 116,
118-119
stretch blind stitch for, 117
tension adjustment for, 117
thread for, 117
decorative,
with added trim, 124
fagoted, 124
hemstitched, 94-96, 122
with narrow ribbon, 122-123
with single-needle stitching, 123
with tucks, 123-124
with twin-needle pintucks, 122
with twin-needle stitching, 63,
122
machine adjustments for, 120, 125
narrow,
at adjoining sides (corner),
136-137
common mistakes in, 132
continuous, 136
curved, 136
ending, 134
fabric for, 128
at facings, 135
guiding, 131-133
with hemstitched handkerchief
edge, 140-141
with picot edge, 140
presser feet for, 128-129
with scalloped edge, 140
with shell edge, 139-140
over seams, 133-134
with specialty stitches, 137-141
stabilizers for, 129

starting, 130
starting, at corner, 133
uses for, 128
See also Hems.
Hems:
with added trim, 124
add-on, with fagoting, 124
curved, 117
depth of, 117
double-fold hemstitched, 94-96, 122
folding fabric for, 118
lengthening, 120-124
with added trim, 125
with growth tucks, 125
with ruffles, 125
measuring, 118
with narrow ribbon, 122-123
pinning, 118
pintuck, 122
pressing, 120
with shell tucks, 124
single-fold hemstitched, 94, 122
with single-needle decorative
stitching, 123
tapered, method for shortening, 125
with tucks, 123-124
with twin-needle decorative
stitching, 122
See also Hemming. Re-hemming.
Hemstitching:
applications for, 68, 81-96
for appliquéing, 87-88
with built-in stitches, 72-76
corded,
appliqué cord for, 76
for attaching lace, 94
cord for, 76
double wing needles with, 70-71
ending, 79
presser feet for, 76-77
stabilizer for, 77
starting, 79
at corners, 79-81
cross stitch for, 73
on curves, 81
daisy stitch for, 73
as decorative topstitch, 82
on difficult fabrics, tips for, 98-99
double wing-needle adjoining rows
method for, 70-71
fabric for, 68
on facings, 82-84
fil tiré, 85-86
as finish for raw edges, 105
four-sided hemstitch for, 73, 79, 85-86
hand vs. machine, 68

for hemming, 94-96
with lace, 88-94
machine settings for, 147-148
needles for, 68, 96
Parisian hemstitch for, 73, 77, 84-85
picot stitch for, 72, 73, 77, 84-85
on plackets, 82-84
on purchased garments, 81-82
Rhodes hemstitch for, 73, 85-86
single wing-needle adjoining rows
method for, 71-72
stabilizer for, 69
tension for, 69
thread for, 68
on tucks, 87
Turkish hemstitch for, 73, 79, 85-86
Venetian hemstitch for, 73, 78, 85
withdrawn threads with, 68, 71, 72,
75-76
zigzag stitch for, 71-72
Herringbone stitch, for fagoting, 102
Honeycomb stitch, for fagoting, 102

I

Index cards, as machine-setup reference,
33, 34

L

Lace:
with cord or cordlike heading,
attachment methods for, 93-94
edging, attachment methods for,
90-93
for fagoting, 107
hemstitched, 88-94
lace for, 89
needles for, 89
insertion, attachment methods for,
89-90, 93-94
side-by-side adjoining, attachment
method for, 93-94
stabilizers for, 107
Lighting, at sewing machine, 39

M

Markers, fabric, selecting, 38-39
Marking:
crease lines as, 28-29
dots vs. lines as, 28
stitching as, 28
Measuring:
with graph paper, 34
with ruler or seam gauge, 34

Metric conversion, chart for, 30
Multiple-zigzag stitch:
    for fagoting, 102
    for shadow work, 61

N

Narrow hemmers:
    described, 17-18
    types of, 128-129
Needle plates:
    guidelines on, 30
    as sewing guides, 29
    straight-stitch, 24
Needle position, changing, 30
Needles:
    for appliqué, 50
    for blind hemming, 117
    for built-in hemstitches, 72
    for buttonholes, 22
    for decorative edges, 44
    Denim, 24
    double wing, 55, 70
    embroidery, 11
    for hemstitching, 68-69
    Jeans, 24
    for lightweight fabrics, 22
    for pintucks, 58
    for shadow work, 61
    Sharp, 11, 24
    size designations of, 12
    specialty twin-needles, 55
    storage for, 12
    testing, in machine, 55, 68
    triple, 55
    twin, 54-55
    Universal, 11, 24
    wing, 68
Notebook, for samples, 8

O

Overcasting stitch, for fagoting, 102

P

Parisian hemstitch:
    for appliquéd edges, 87
    for built-in hemstitching, 73
    corded, 77
    for hemstitched edge, 140-141
    machine settings for, 147-148
    for multiple adjoining rows, 84
    for tucks, 87

Picot stitch:
    for appliquéd edges, 87
    corded, 77
    for hemstitched handkerchief edge, 140-141
    for hemstitching, 72-73
    for multiple adjoining rows, 84
    for tucks, 87
Pin stitch. See Parisian hemstitch.
Pincushions, magnetic, and computerized machines, 146
Pintucks, twin-needle:
    applications for, 57-58
    corded, 59-60
    fabric for, 58, 60-61
    measuring and marking for, 58-59
    needles for, 58
    presser feet for, 58, 65
    pressing, 65
    securing, 64
    stitch direction of, 65
    tension adjustments for, 57, 64
    thread for, 58
Piping, making and applying, 38
Point de Paris. See Parisian hemstitch.
Presser feet:
    for blind hemming, 117
    blind-hem, 16, 17
    for built-in hemstitching, 73
    buttonhole, 16, 17, 22
    for corded edges, 45
    for corded hemstitching, 76-77
    as fagoting guides, 103
    and feed-dog compatibility, 14
    with flat vs. indented underside, 13
    interchanging, 15
    for lightweight fabrics, 22
    multiple-cord, 16-17
    narrow-hem, 17-18
    for narrow hems, 128-129
    open-toe, 16
    pintuck, 18
    for pintucks, 58
    satin-stitch, 13
    as sewing guides, 29-30
    for shadow work, 61
    short-shank, 15
    straight-stitch, 13, 14
    for twin-needle stitching, 56
    zigzag, 13
        as straight-stitch foot substitute, 14
Puckering, prevention of:
    in lengthwise pintucks on difficult fabrics, 60-61
    in lengthwise stitching, 7

and sewing taut, 19
and stitch length, 18
with straight-stitch feet, 13-14
and tension, 20-21

R

Re-hemming, invisible, 121-122
Rhodes hemstitch:
    for built-in hemstitching, 73
    for machine-made fil tiré, 85-86
Rolled hemmers. See Narrow hemmers.

S

Sample notebook, as reference tool, 8
Satin stitch, and machine jams, 23-24
Scallops:
    as finish for raw edges, 105
    See also Edging scallop stitch. Tracery scallop stitch.
Seam guides, discussed, 31-32
Seams:
    French, 37
    thick, 40
Serpentine stitch, for shadow work, 61
Sewing machines:
    automatic stop feature for, 142
    balancing mechanism for, 143
    brand-specific features on, 144
    cleaning, 6, 145
    embroidery capabilities for, 143
    feeding mechanisms for, 142
    instruction manual for, 144
    light for, 143
    low-bobbin warning for, 143
    maintenance for, 145
    mirror imaging on, 143
    needle-down feature for, 142
    needle-position change capability for, 143
    oiling, 6, 145
    portability of, 143
    presser feet for, 144
    programming capability for, 143
    removable table for, 143
    repair of, 145
    reverse button for, 143
    securing option for, 143
    speed reducer for, 143
    stitch capability of, 142
    stitch-length features for, 143
    stitch-width features for, 143
    surge protectors for, 145
    tension mechanisms for, 142
    thread cutter/holder for, 143

transporting, 146
troubleshooting, 6
twin-needle capability for, 143
updatability of, 143
Sewing speed:
for best results, 22
and stitch alignment, 71
and stitch density, 41
Shadow work, twin-needle:
bracket stitch for, 61
corded, 62
fabric for, 61
machine settings for, 147-148
multi-zigzag stitch for, 61
needles for, 61
presser feet for, 61
serpentine stitch for, 61
stabilizer for, 62
stitch width for, 62
thread for, 61
tracery scallop stitch for, 61
Shell hemmers. *See* Narrow hemmers.
Stabilizer:
for appliqué, 50
for buttonholes, 22
for hemstitching, 69, 77
for lightweight fabrics, 22
for narrow hems, 129
for 'no-trim-around' scalloped edge,
48
paper as, disadvised, 19
for picot edge, 46
for shadow work, 62
tearaway, 19
tearing away, 19
for twin-needle stitching, 57
water-soluble, 20
Stitch alignment, balancing, 74, 76
Stitch length:
for built-in hemstitching, 73
for corded edges, 45
discussed, 18
for gathering, 18
for lightweight fabrics, 22
machine settings for, for specific
stitches, 147-148
metric conversion for, 18
for seaming, 18
Stitch width:
for built-in hemstitching, 73
discussed, 18-19
for fagoting, 102
machine settings for, for specific
stitches, 147-148
for shadow work, 62
for twin-needle stitching, 56-57

Stitches:
for built-in hemstitching, 73
for creative appliqué, 50
for decorative edges, 45
for fagoting, 102, 110
for hemming, 117
for hemstitching, 70, 71, 73, 82, 84,
85
for narrow hemming, 128, 137, 139,
140, 141
for shadow work, 61
See also specific stitches.
Stitching:
directional, 40, 65
on small pieces, 35
securing, 35
technique for ending, 33, 35
technique for starting, 33, 35
troubleshooting, for problems, 6
Stretch blind stitch:
for blind hemming, 117
for picot edge, 46, 140
Stretch stitch, for picot edge, 46

T

Taut sewing, to eliminate puckering.
7, 18, 19
Tension:
adjusting, 20-21
bobbin, 20, 25
for buttonholes, 23
described, 20
for hemstitching, 69
for lightweight fabric, 22
machine-to-machine variation in, 25
for twin-needle stitching, 57
upper vs. bobbin, 20
Test samples:
need for, 7
notebook for, 8
Thread:
for appliqué, 49
for blind hemming, 117
for buttonholes, 22
buttonhole twist, 9-10
cordonnet, 9-10
cotton, 9
cotton-wrapped polyester, 9
for decorative edges, 44
for decorative stitching, 8-10
for hemstitching, 68
for lightweight fabrics, 22
machine embroidery cotton, 9
mercerized, 24
metallic, 9

pearl cotton, 10, 45
for pintucks, 58
polyester, 9
rayon, 9
for seaming, 8
for shadow work, 61
topstitching, 9-10
for twin-needle stitching, 56
withdrawn, for hemstitching, 68, 71,
72, 75-76
Threading:
with presser foot up, 10
for twin-needle stitching, 57, 64
Tracery scallop stitch, for shadow work,
61
Troubleshooting, for stitching problems,
6
Tucks:
embellished, 124
as finish for raw edges, 105
growth, 125
hemstitched, 87
Turkish hemstitch:
for built-in hemstitching, 73
over cord or ribbon, 79
for machine-made fil tiré, 85-86
Twin-needle stitching:
applications for, 54, 62-63
cord for, 56
on difficult fabric, 60-61
fabric for, 55-56
for hems, 63
presser feet for, 56
stabilizer for, 57
stitch width for, 56-57
tension for, 57
thread for, 56
threading for, 57, 64
See also Pintucks. Shadow work.

V

Venetian hemstitch:
for built-in hemstitching, 73
corded, 78
for fagoting, 110
for multiple adjoining rows, 85
at corners, 80
for fagoting, 102
machine settings for, 147-148

Z

Zigzag stitch:
for corded edges, 45
for hemstitching, 71

Publisher: Suzanne La Rosa

Acquisitions editor: Jolynn Gower

Publishing coordinator: Sarah Coe

Editors: Eileen Hanson, Mary Galpin Barnes, Ruth Dobsevage

Designer/layout artist: Jodie Delohery

Illustrator: Rosalie Vaccaro

Photographers: Scott Phillips (black and white photos),
              Marcus Tullis (color photos)

Stylist: Sheila Shulman

Typeface: Goudy

Paper: 70-lb. Somerset Matte

Printer: Quebecor Printing/Hawkins, New Canton, Tennessee